AF251523

HIDDEN TREASURES

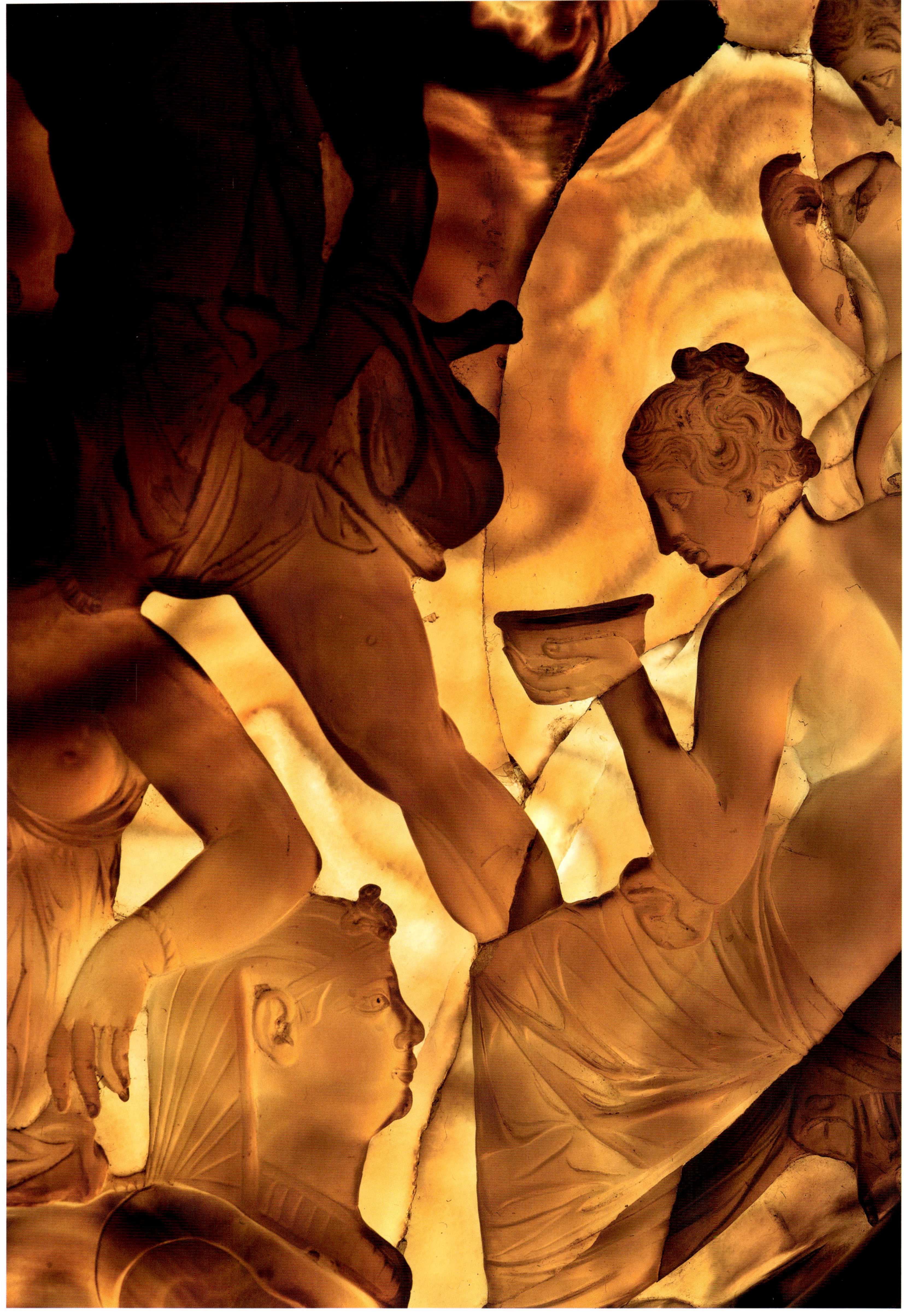

The Farnese Cup

Valeria Sampaolo | Luigi Spina

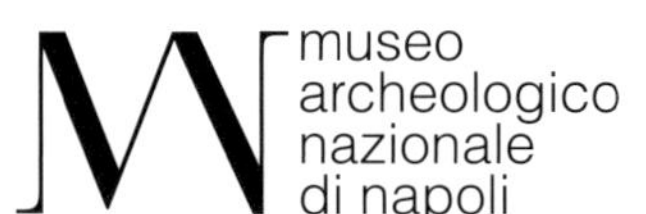

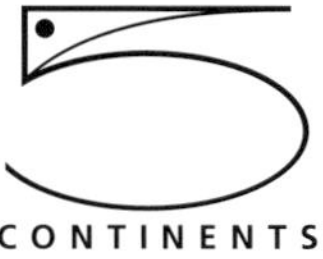

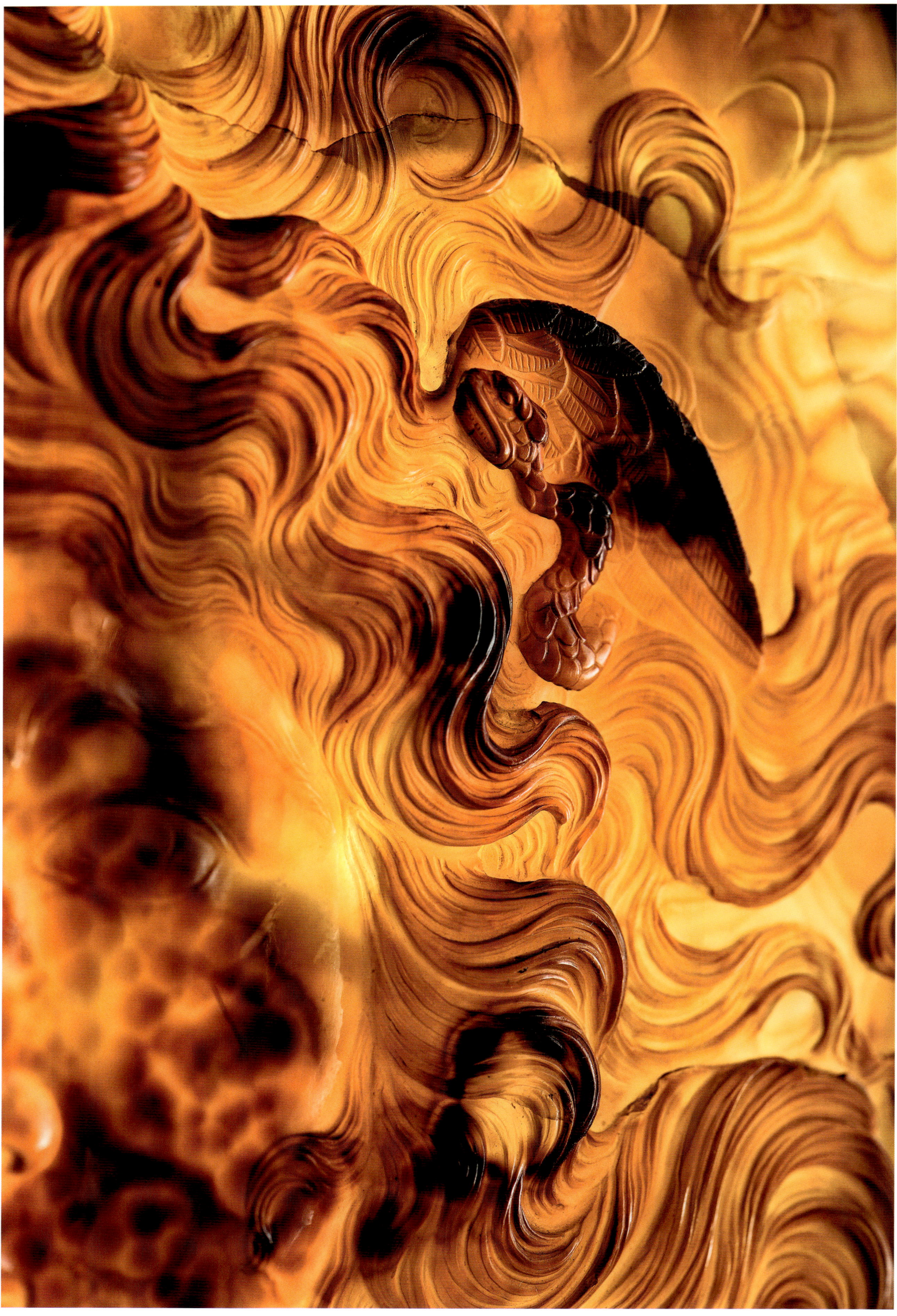

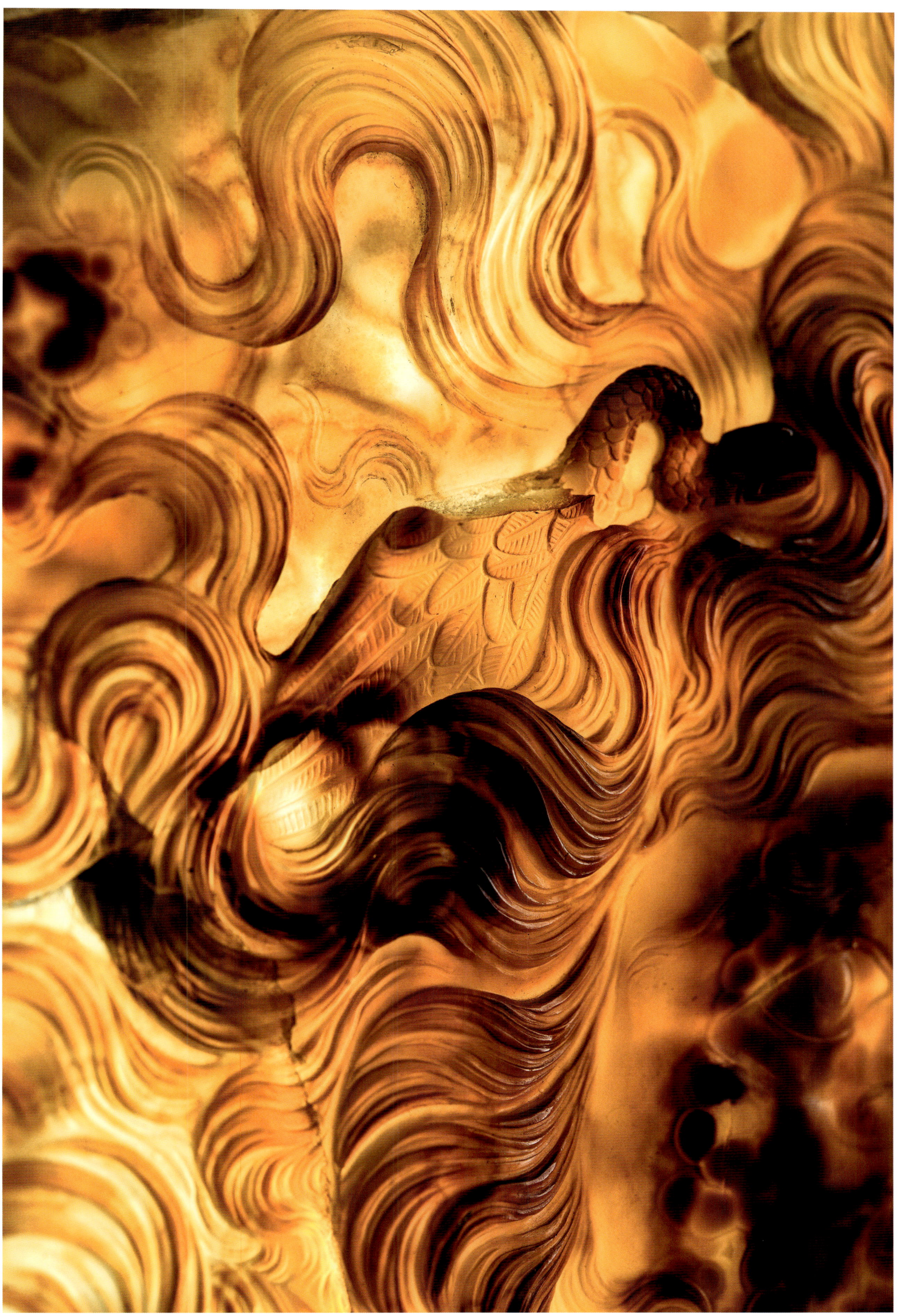

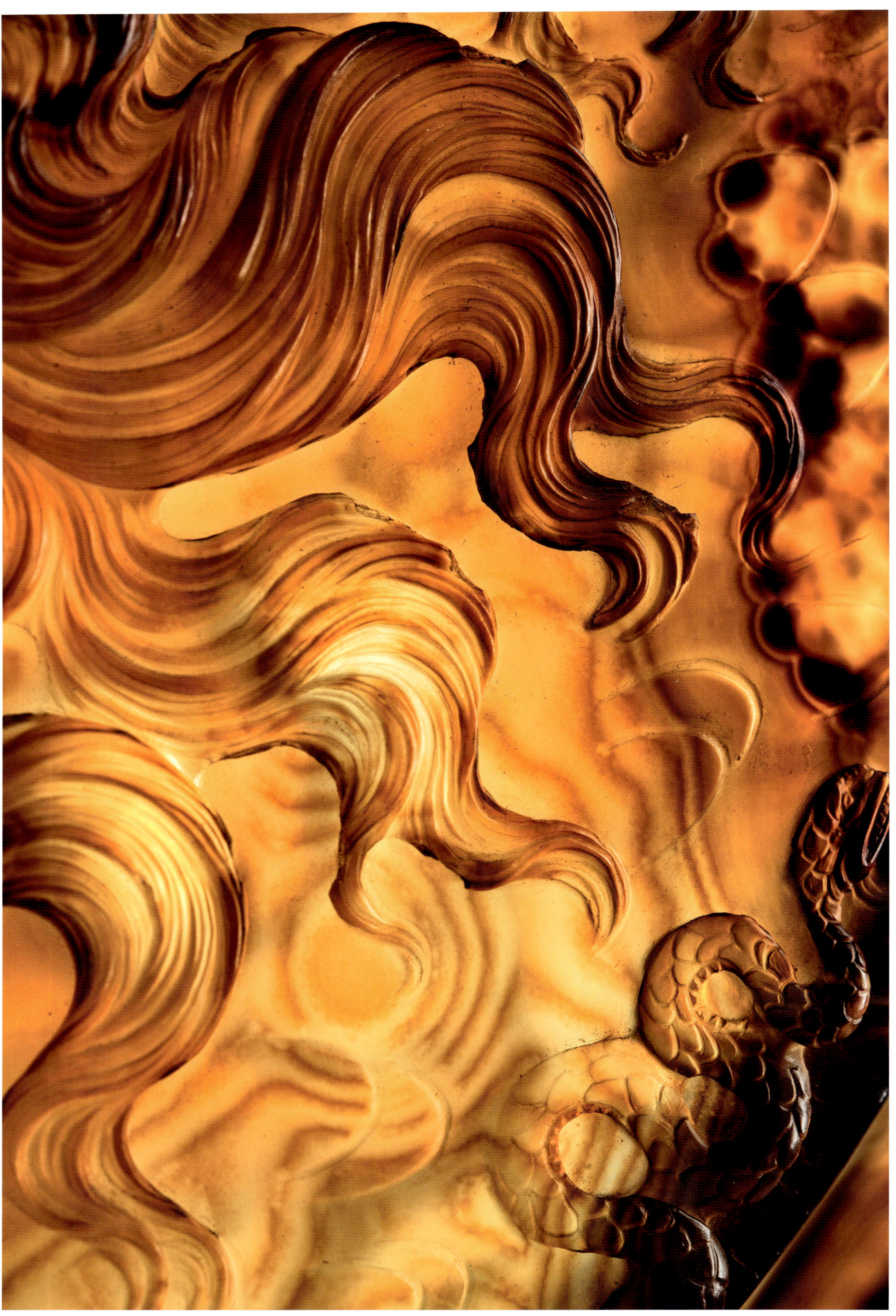

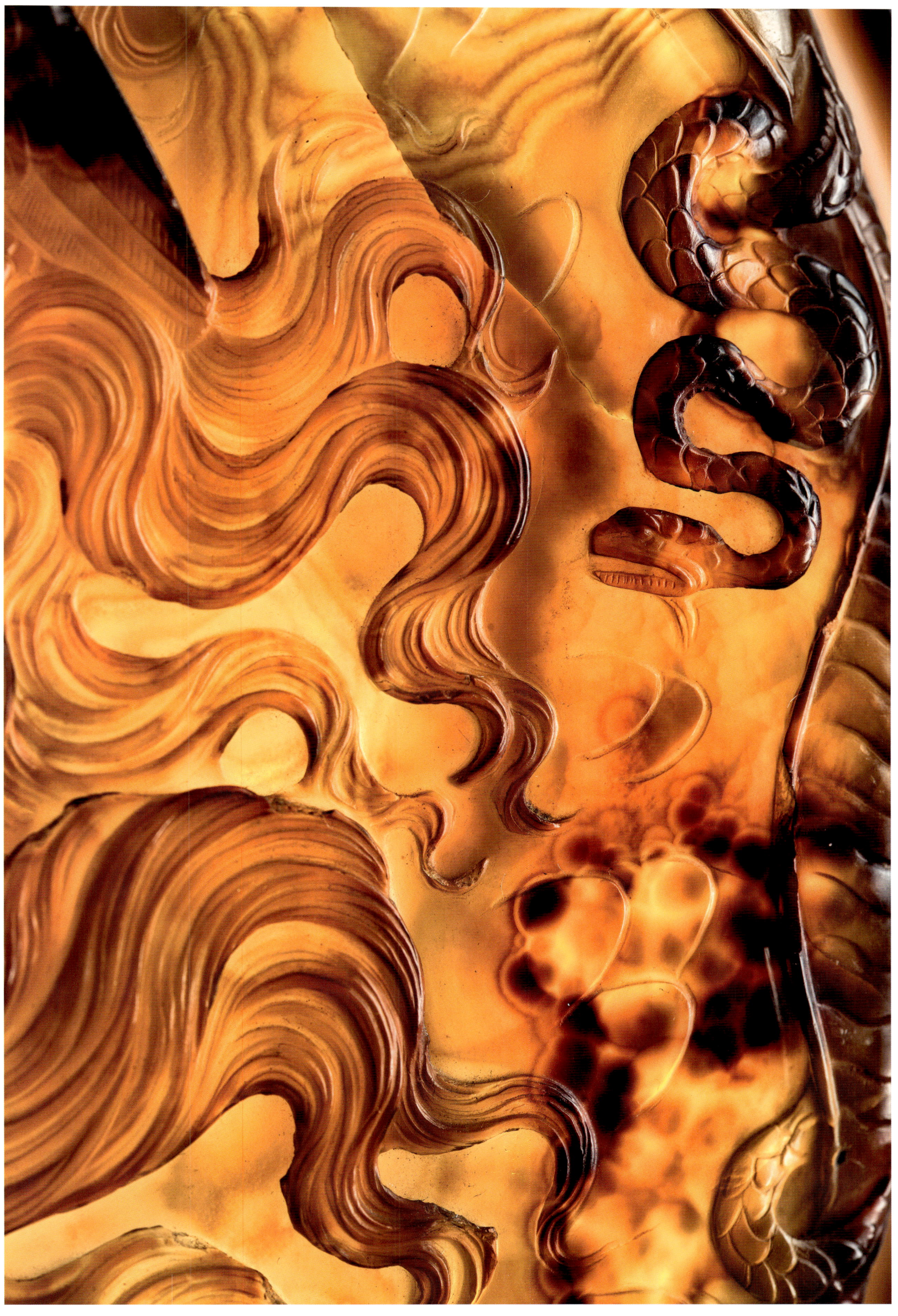

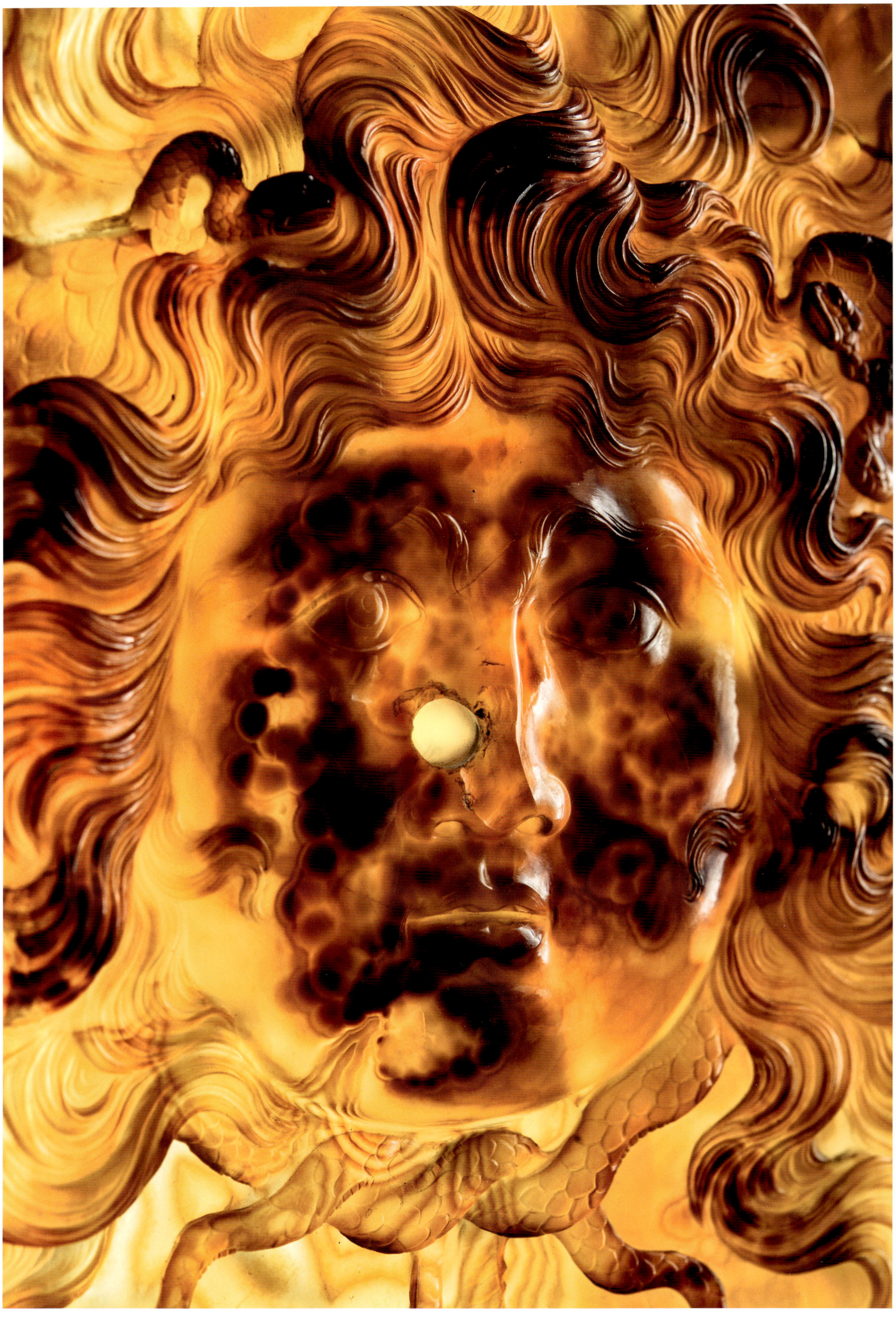

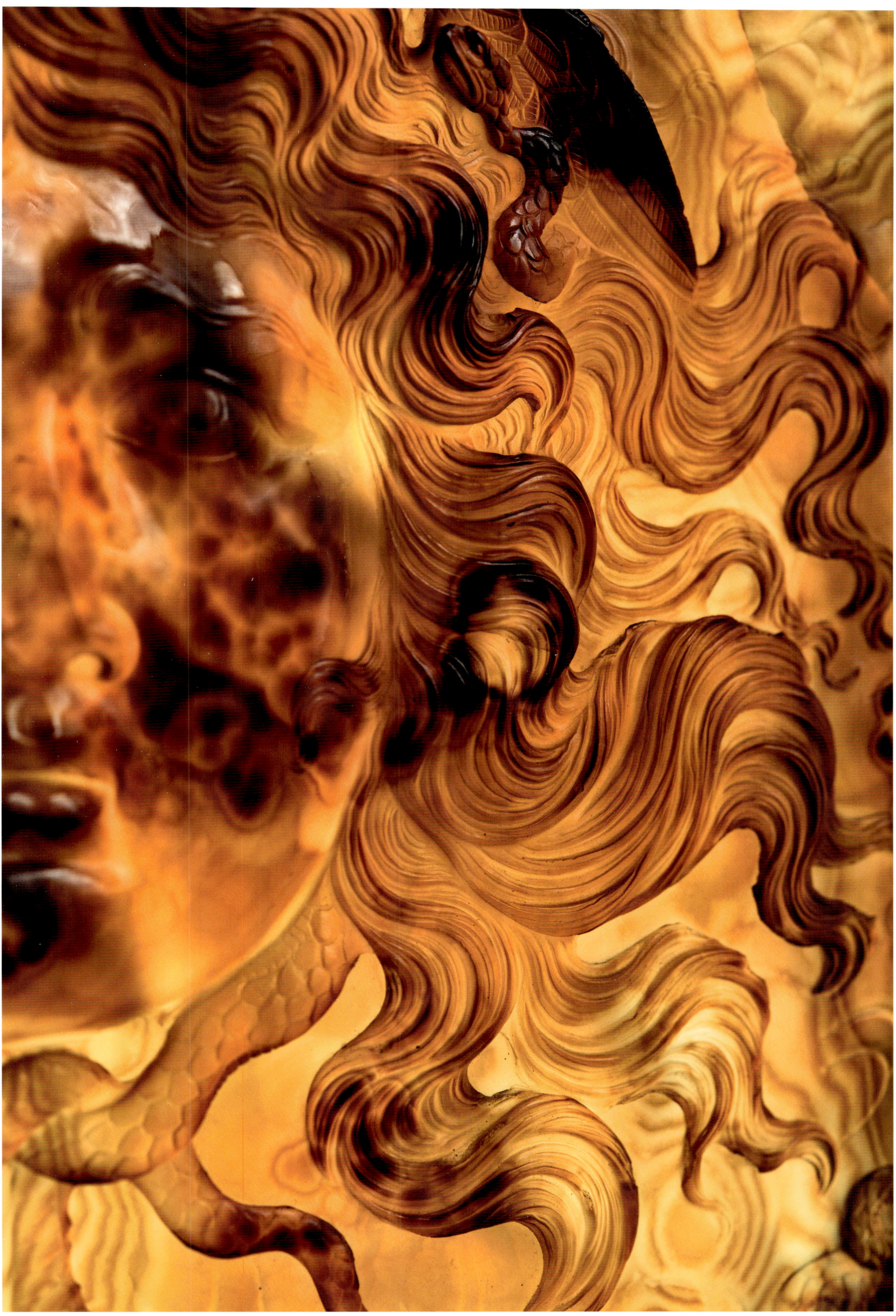

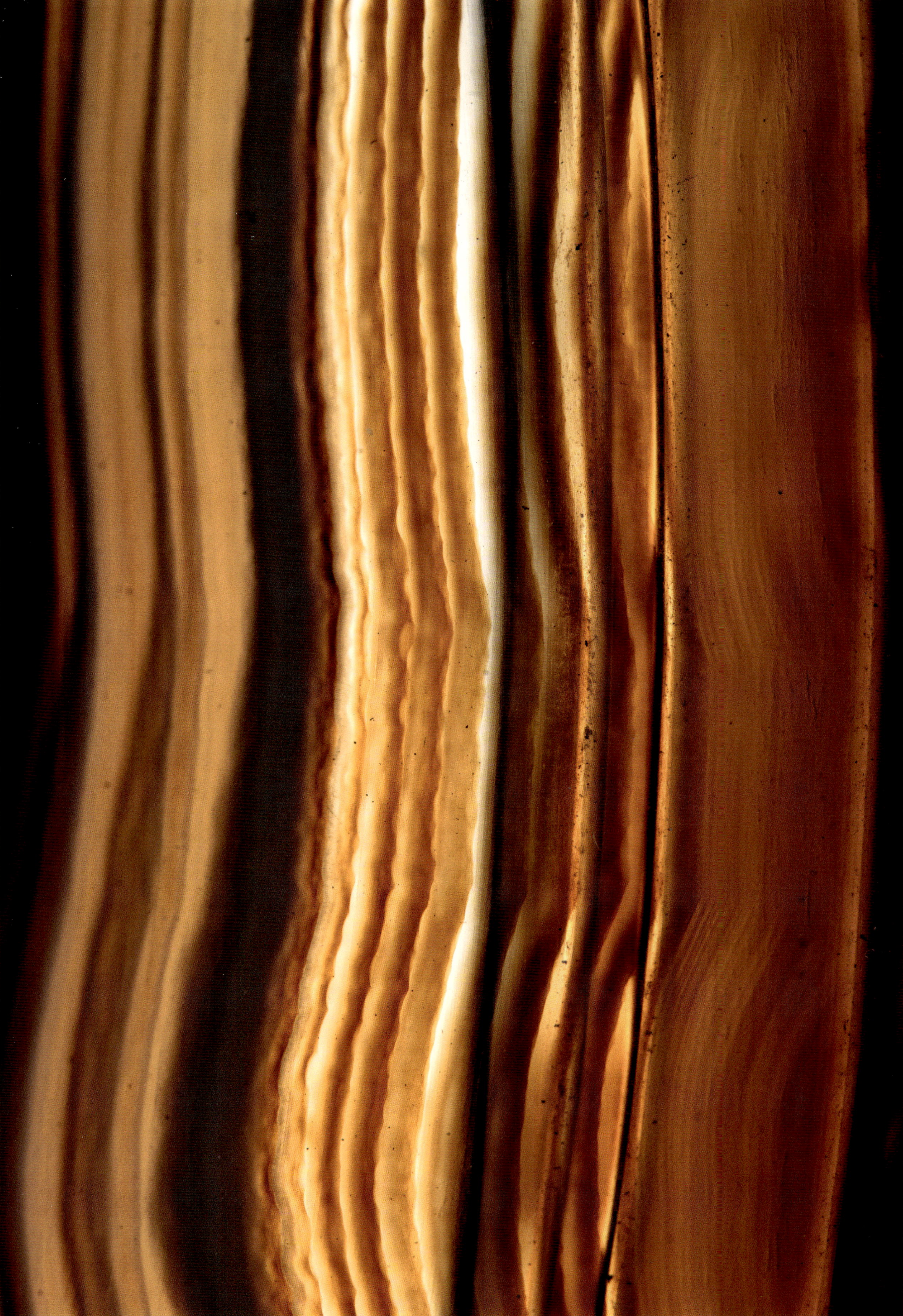

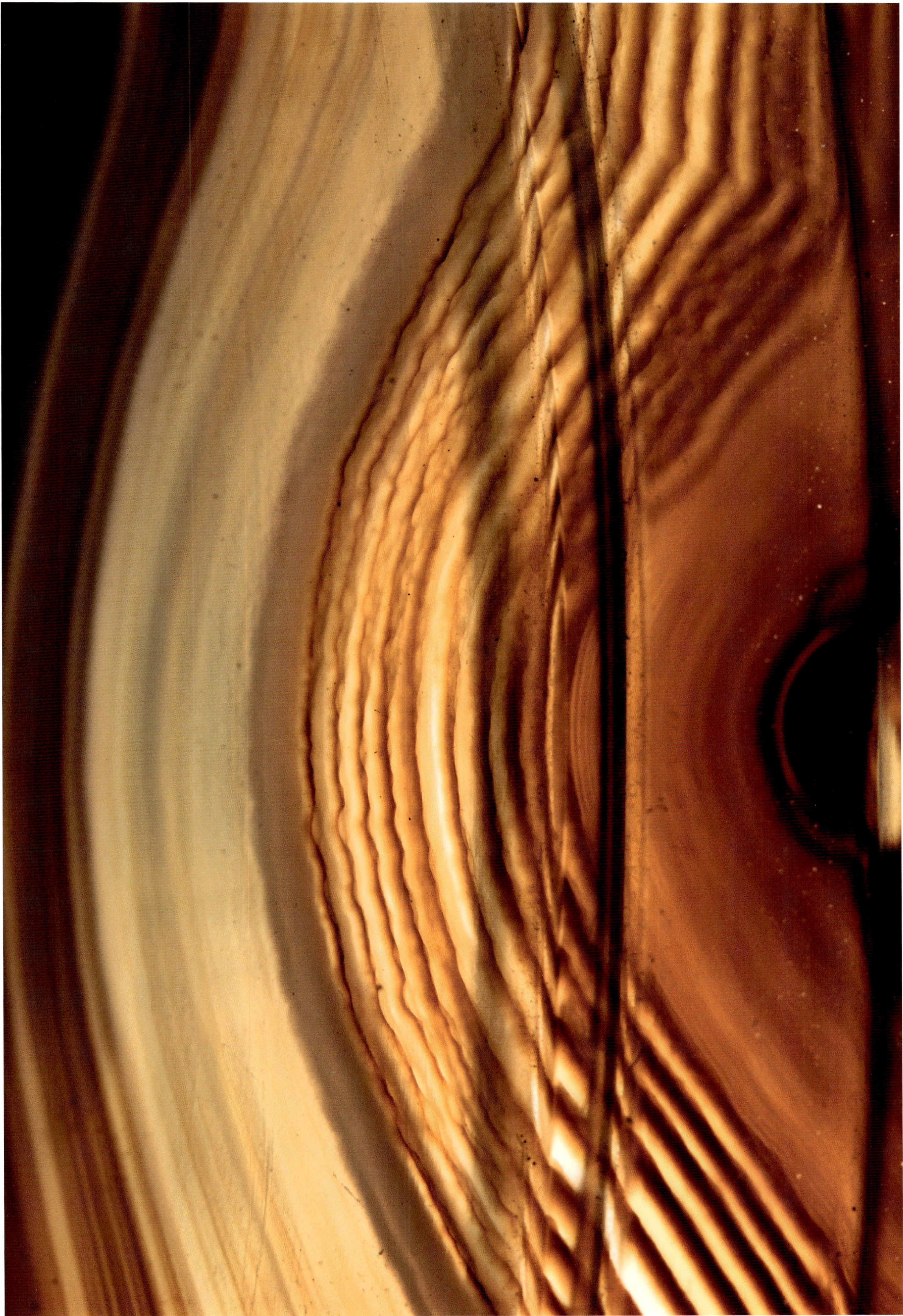

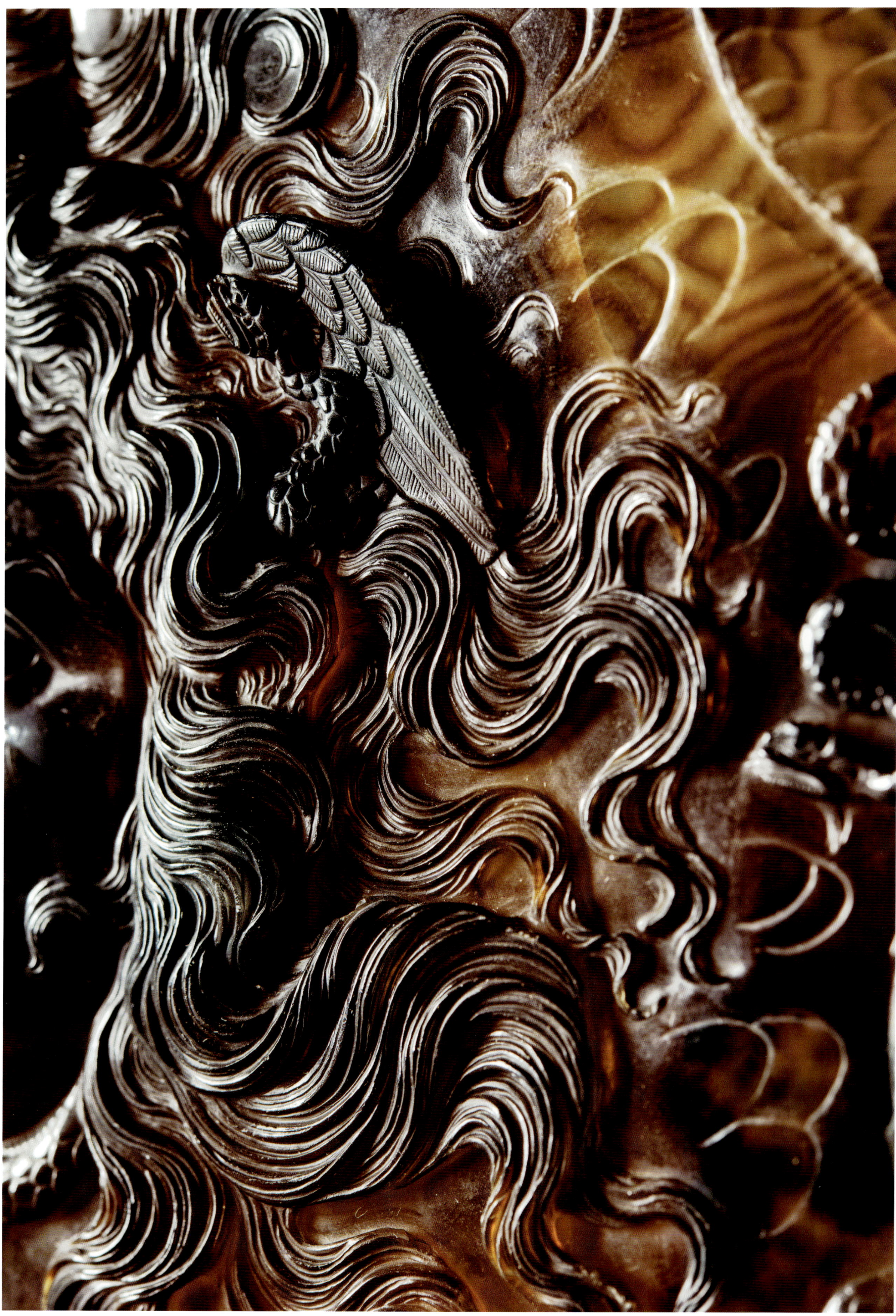

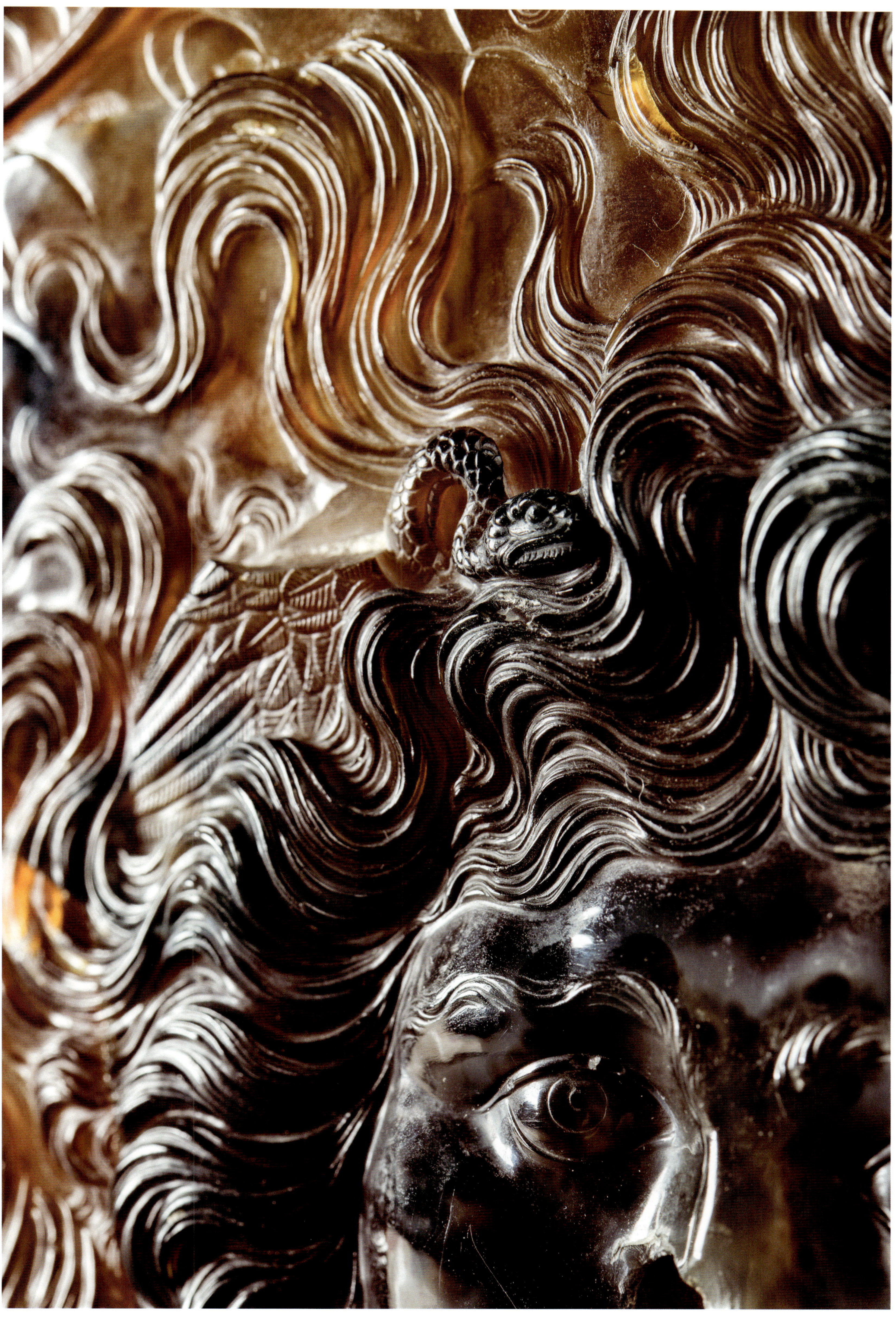

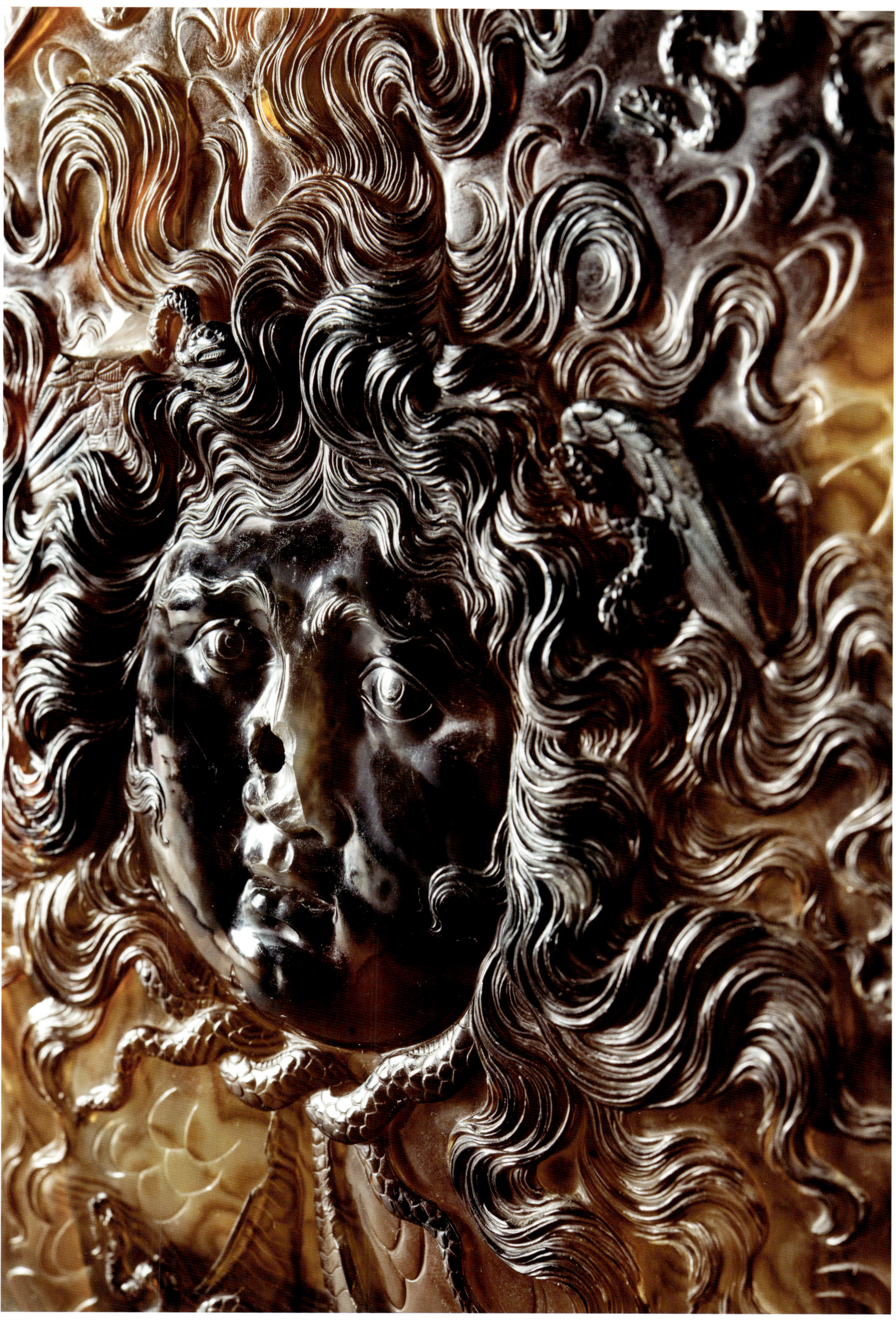

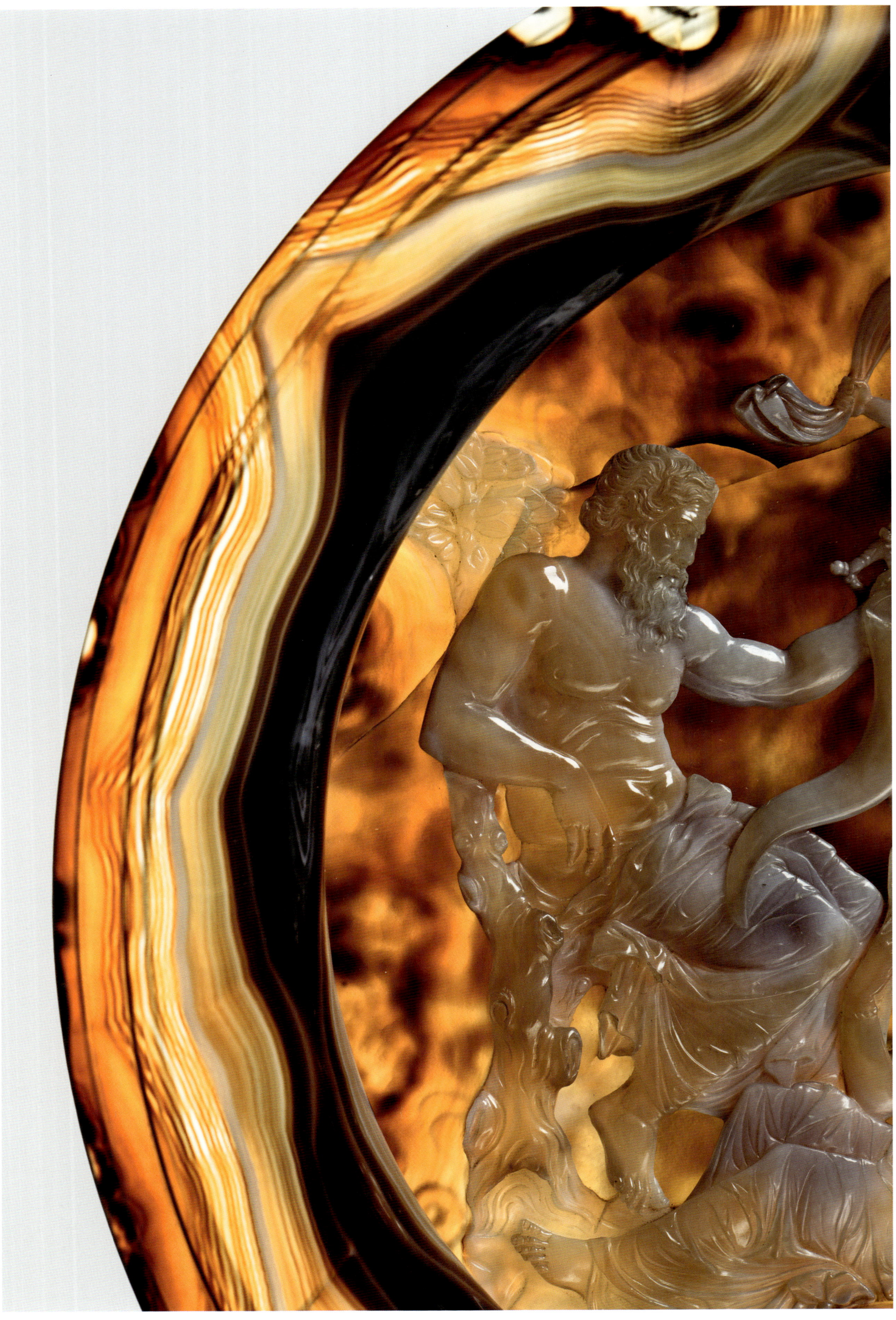

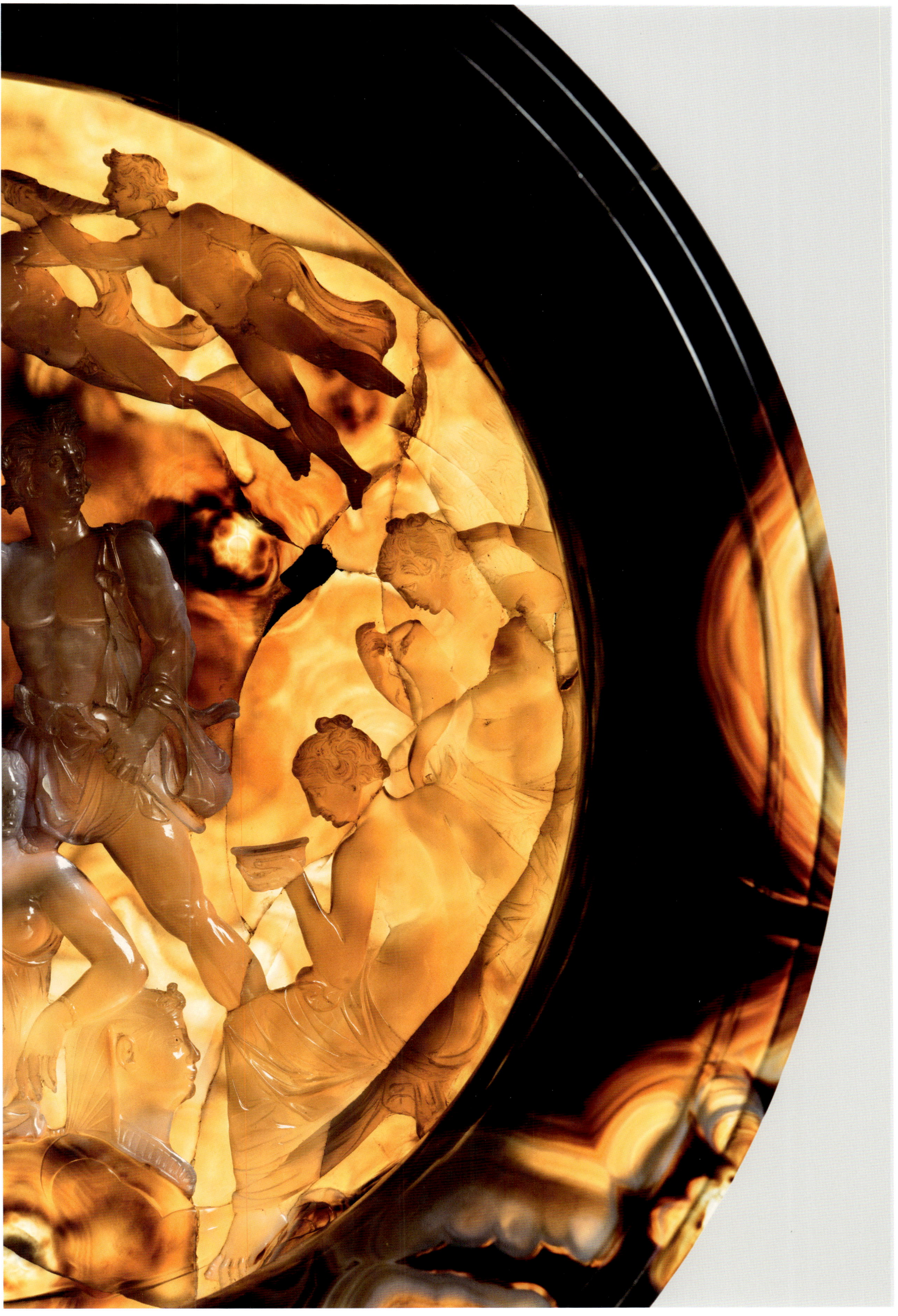

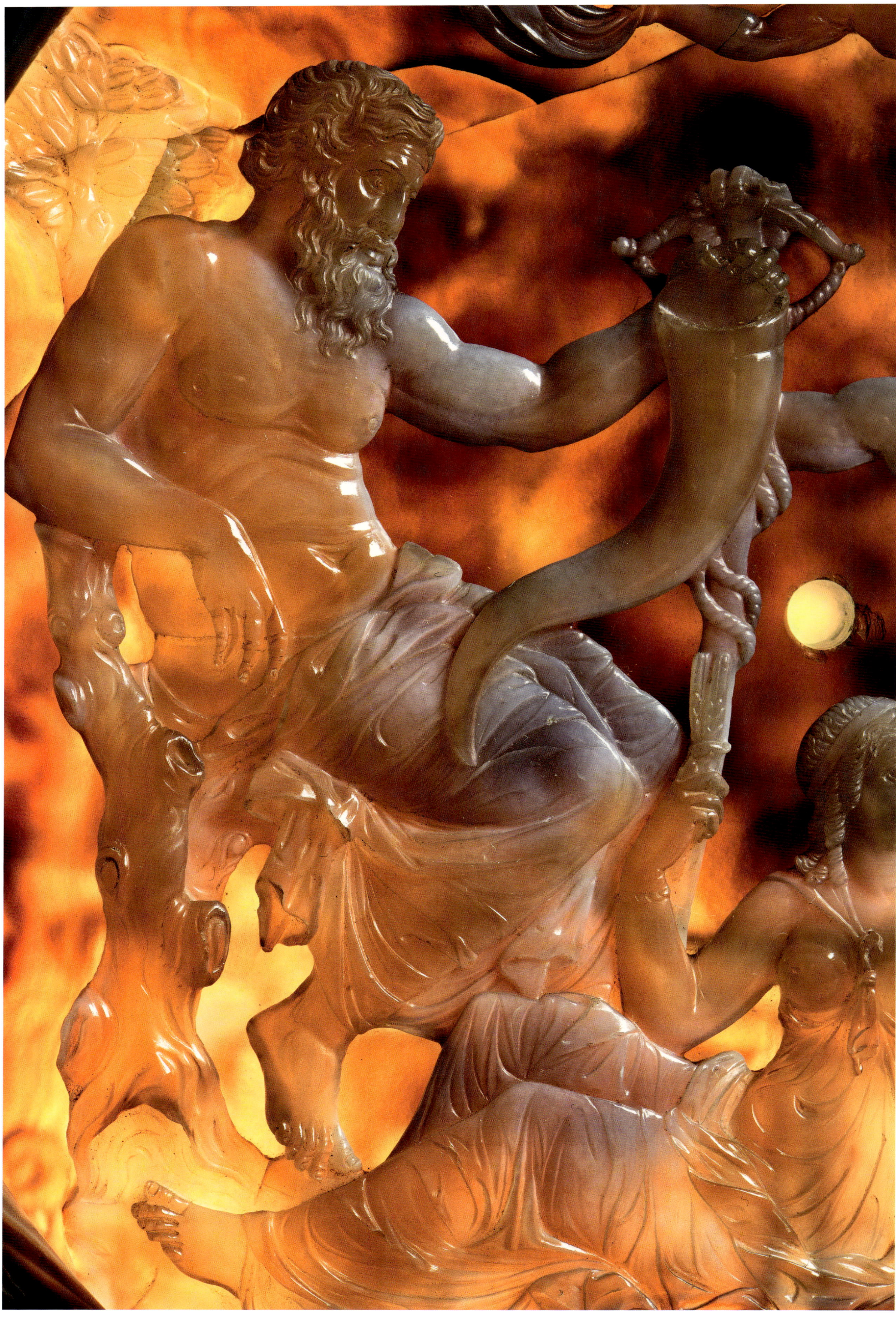

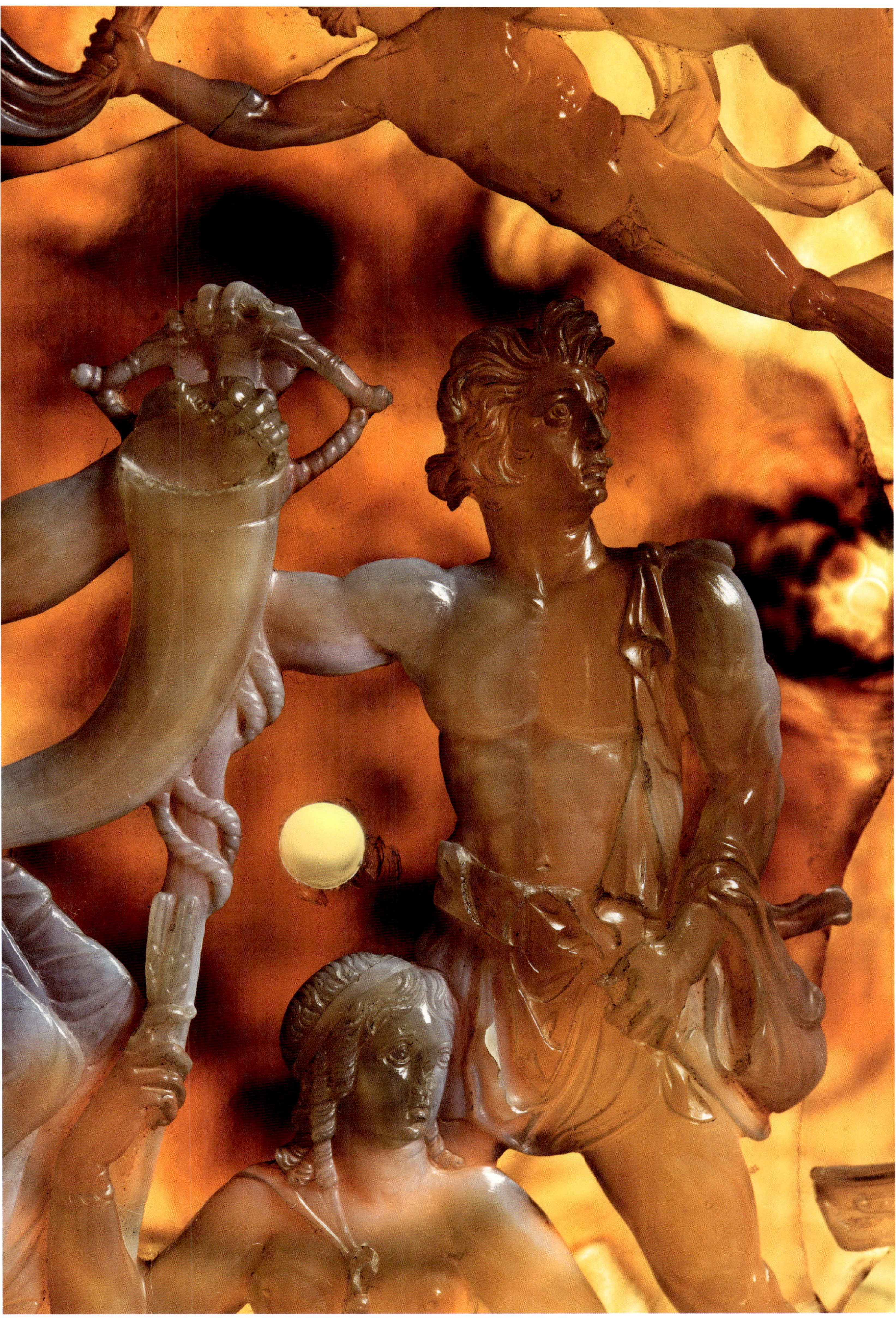

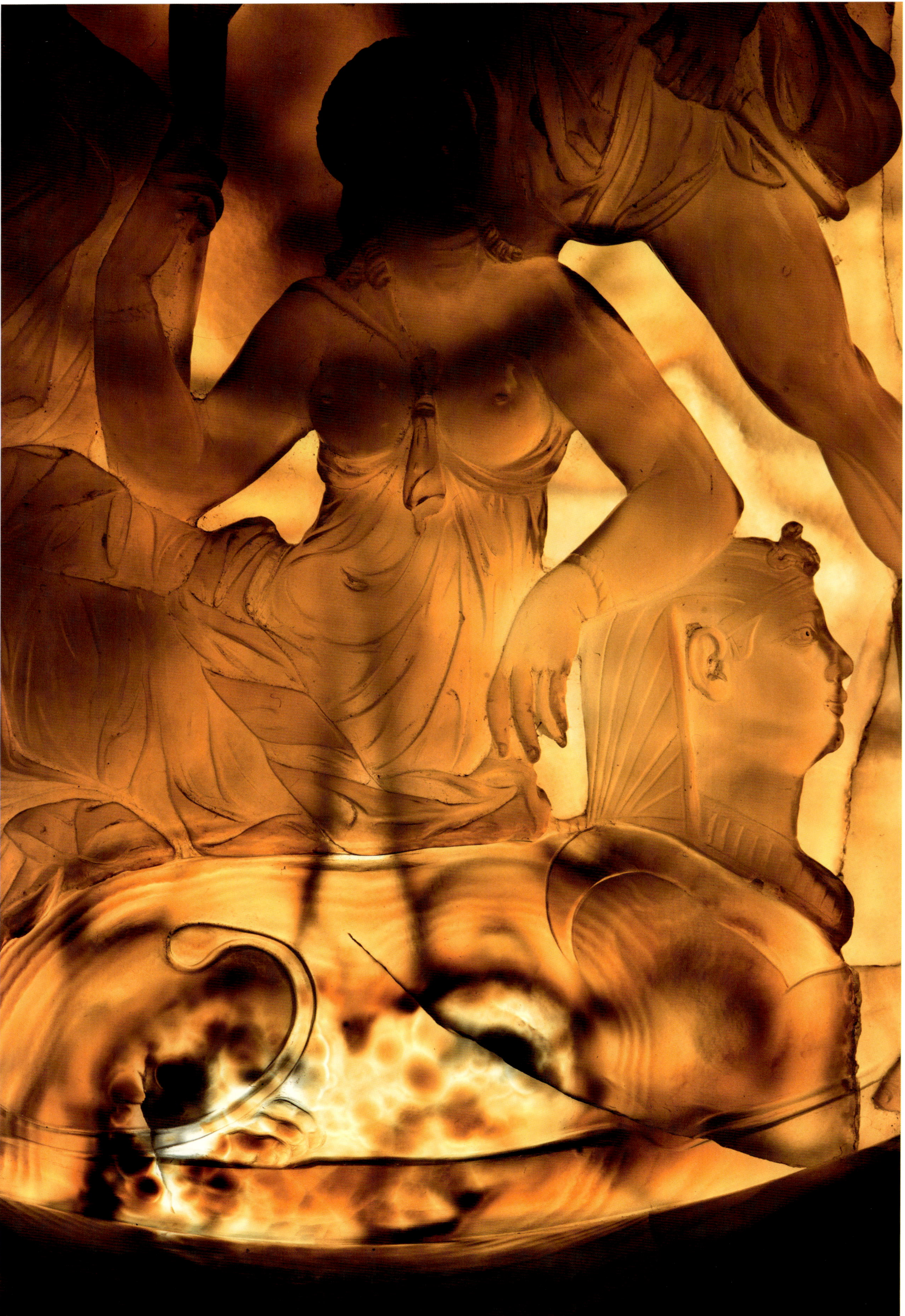

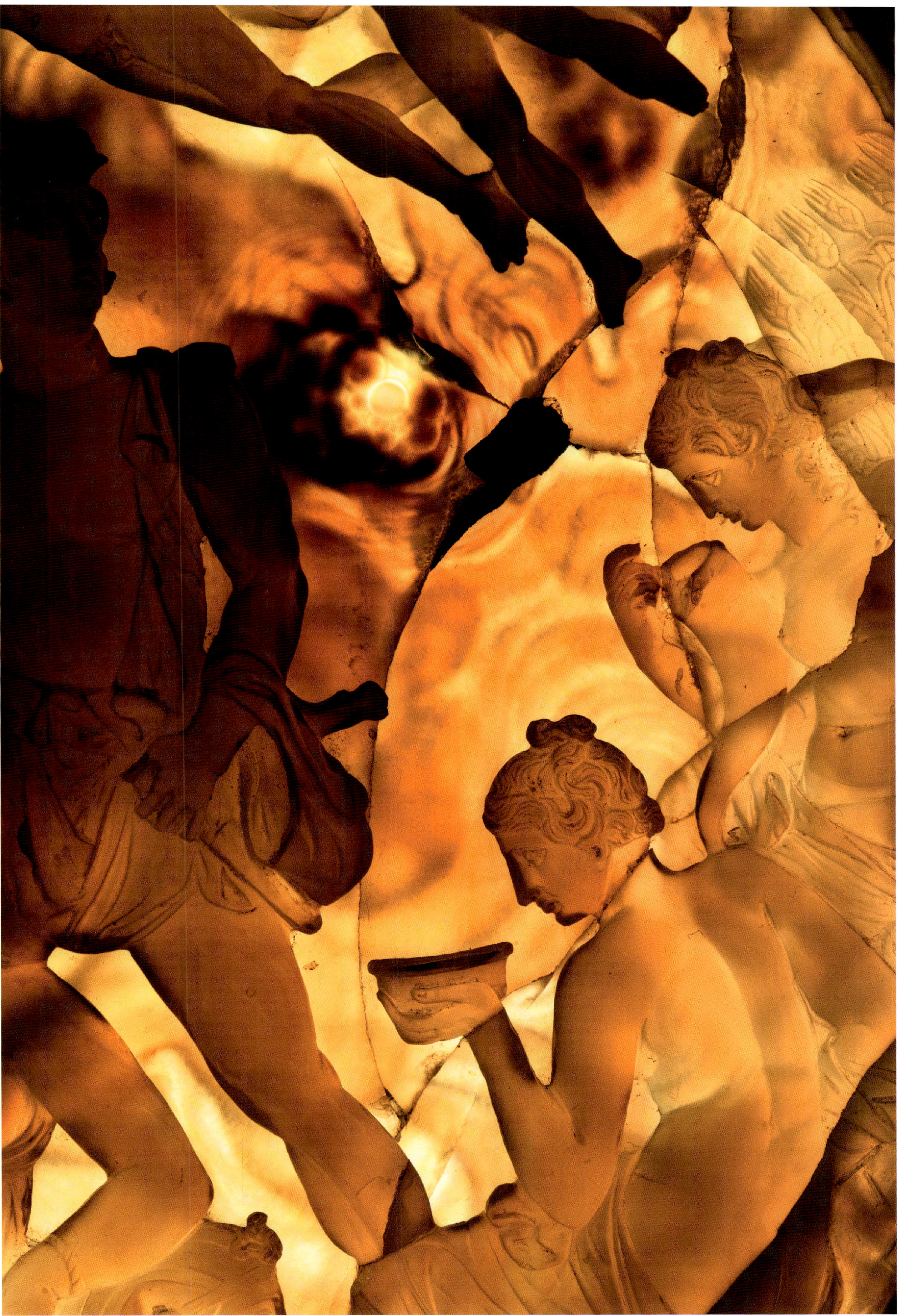

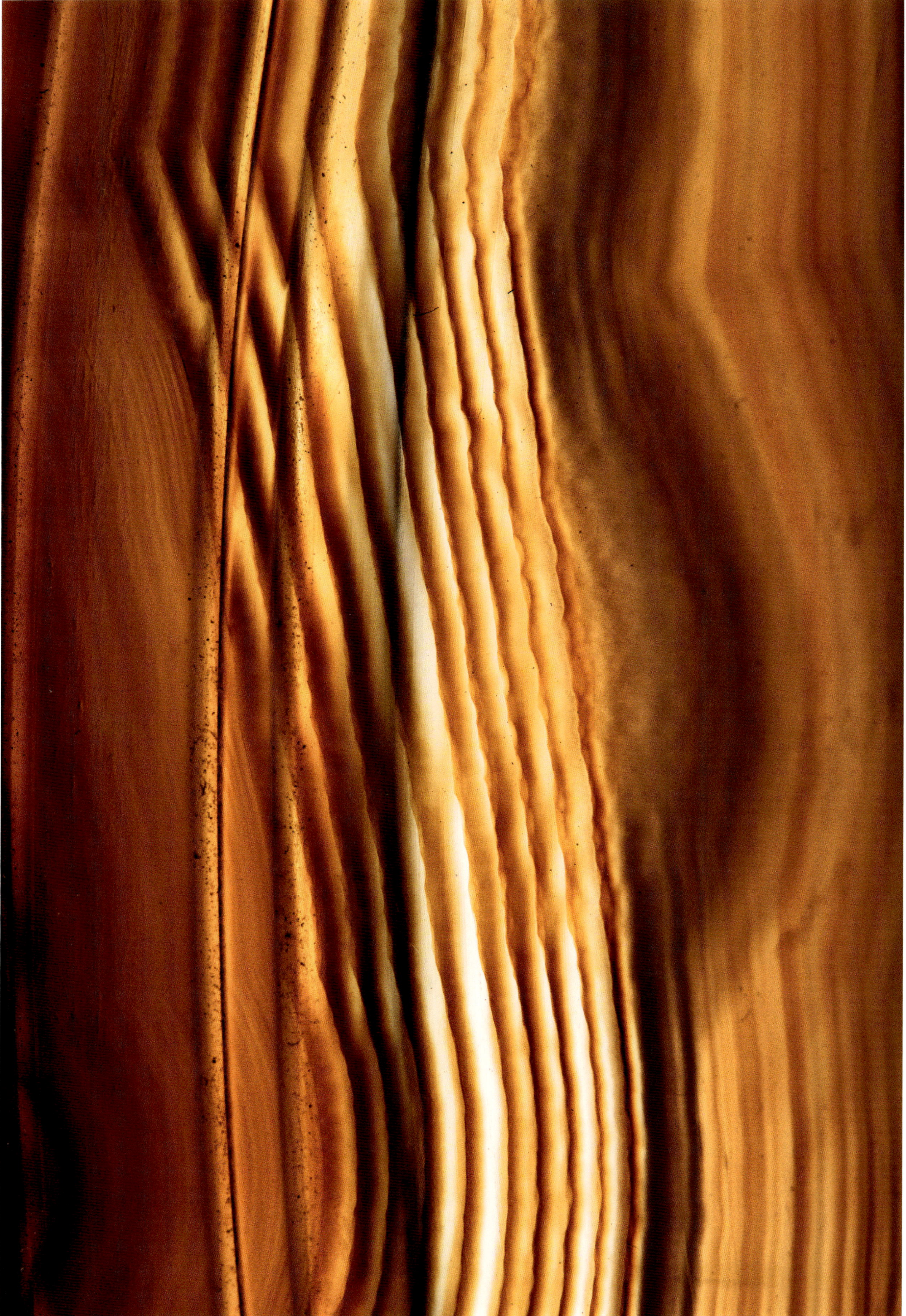

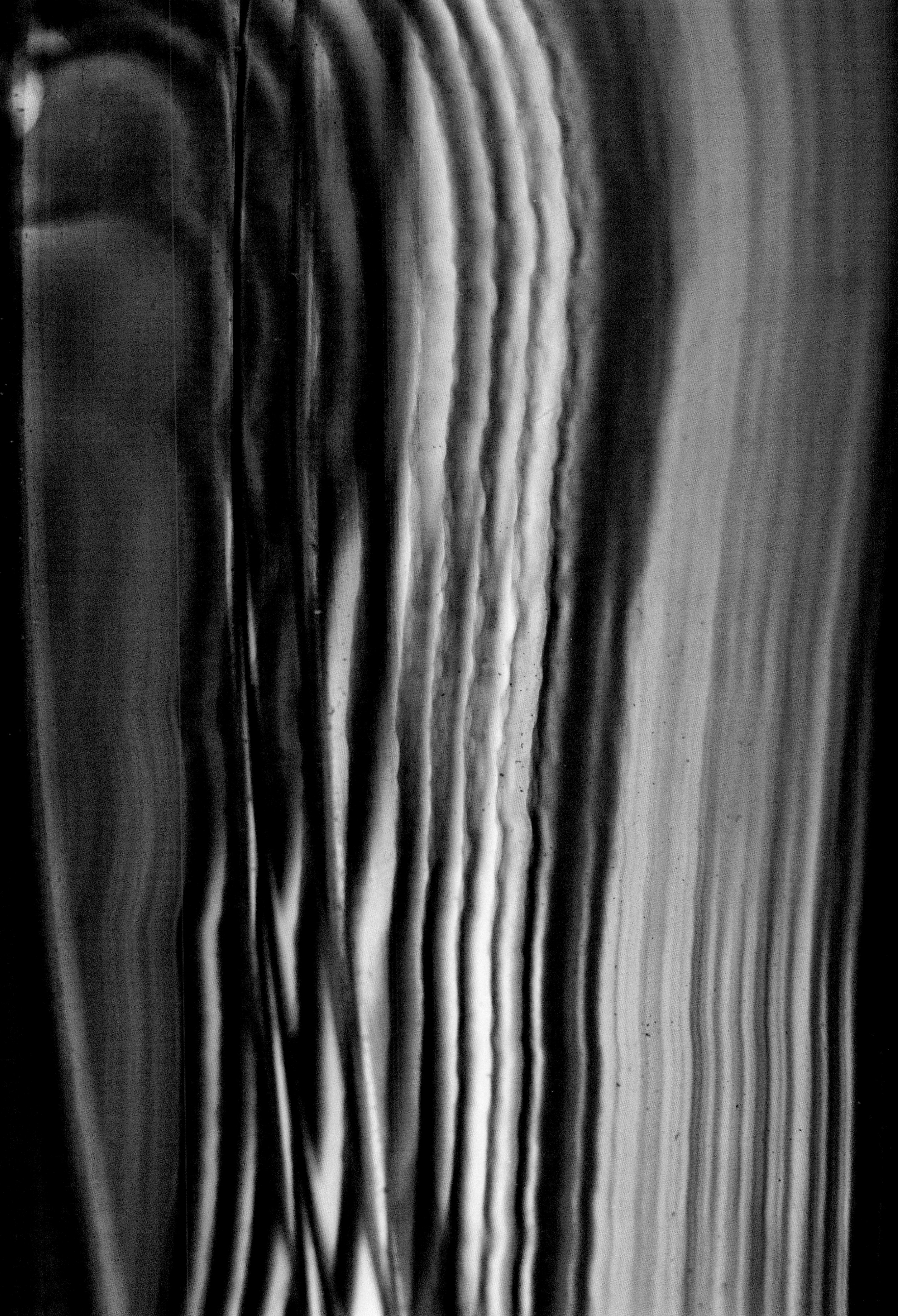

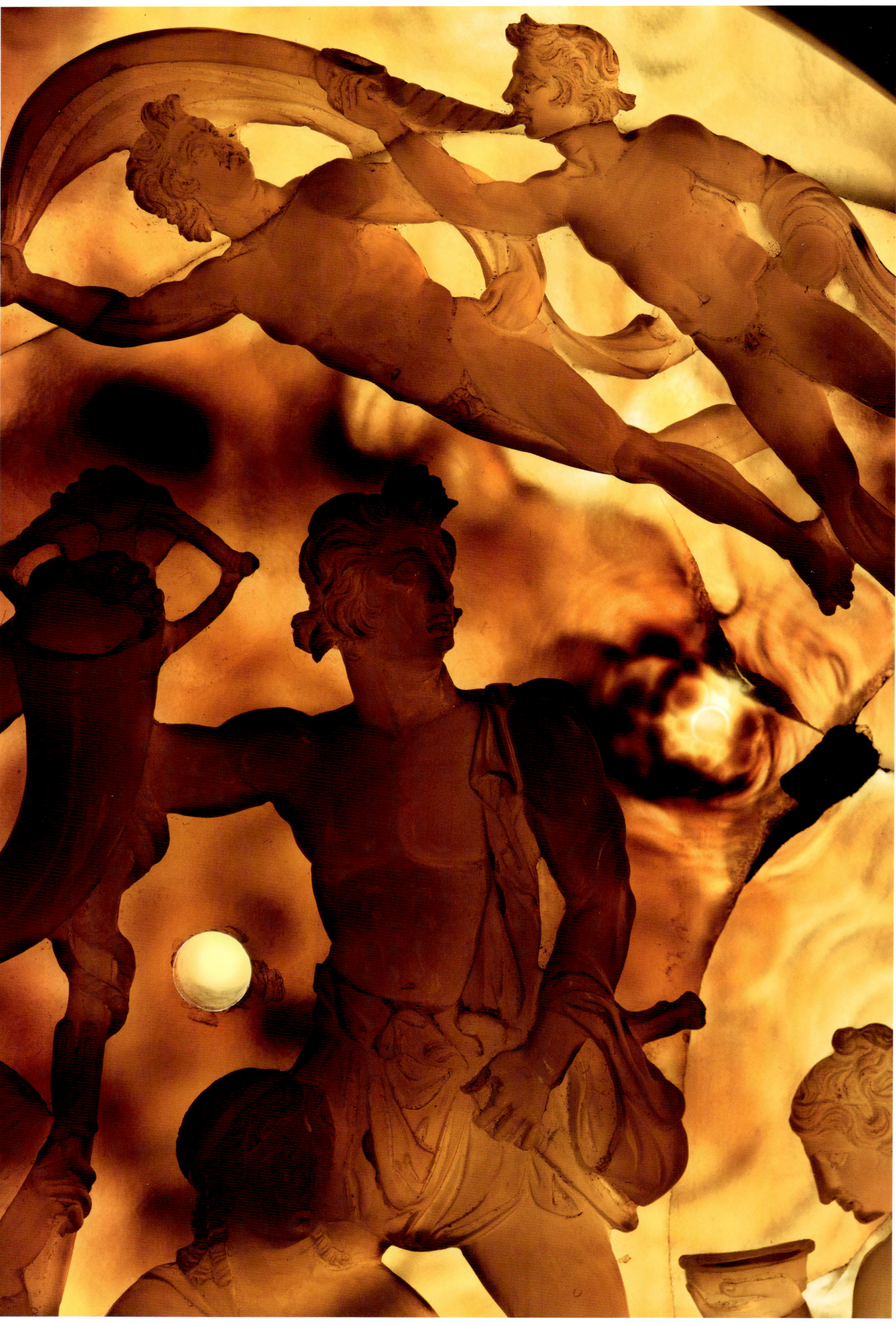

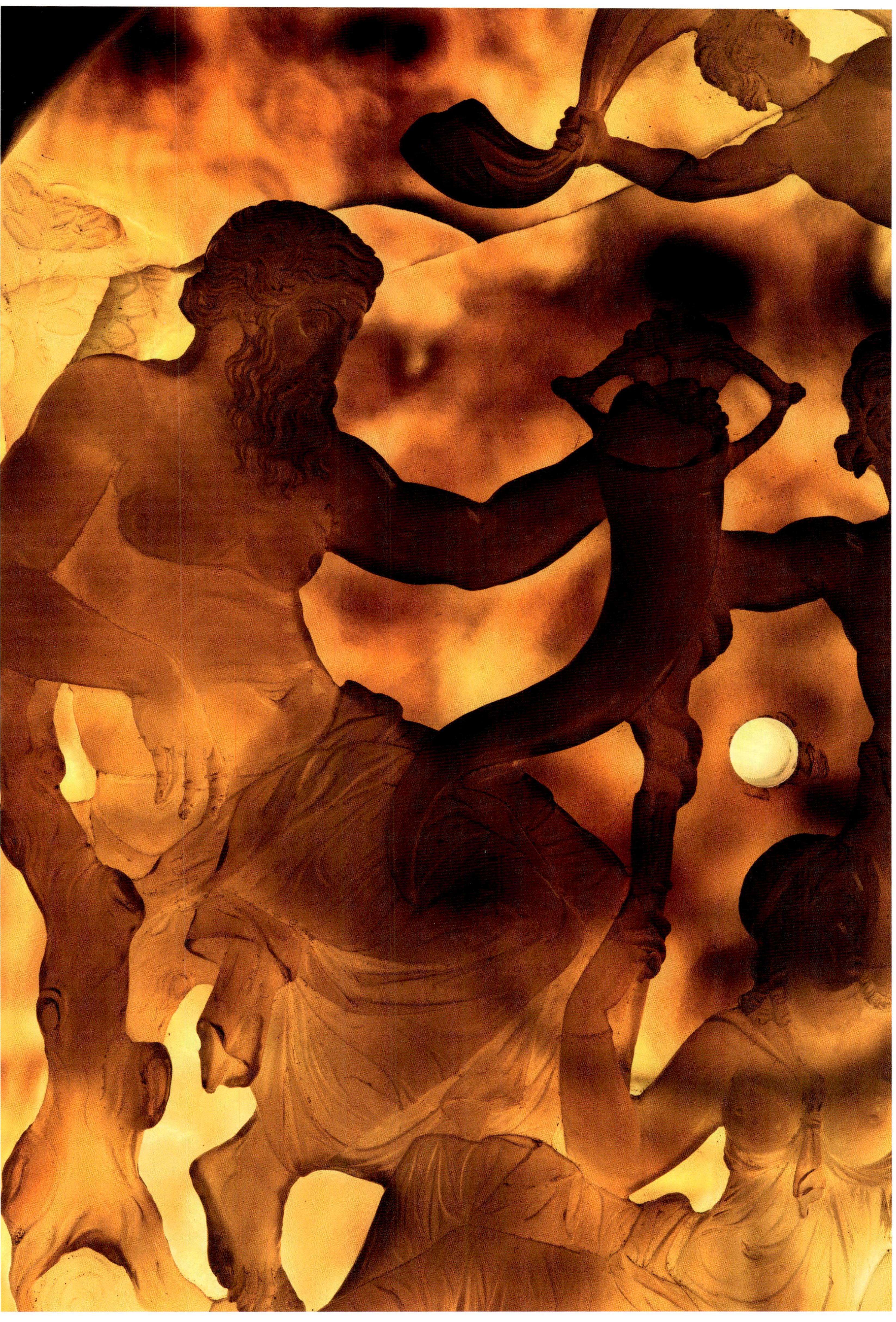

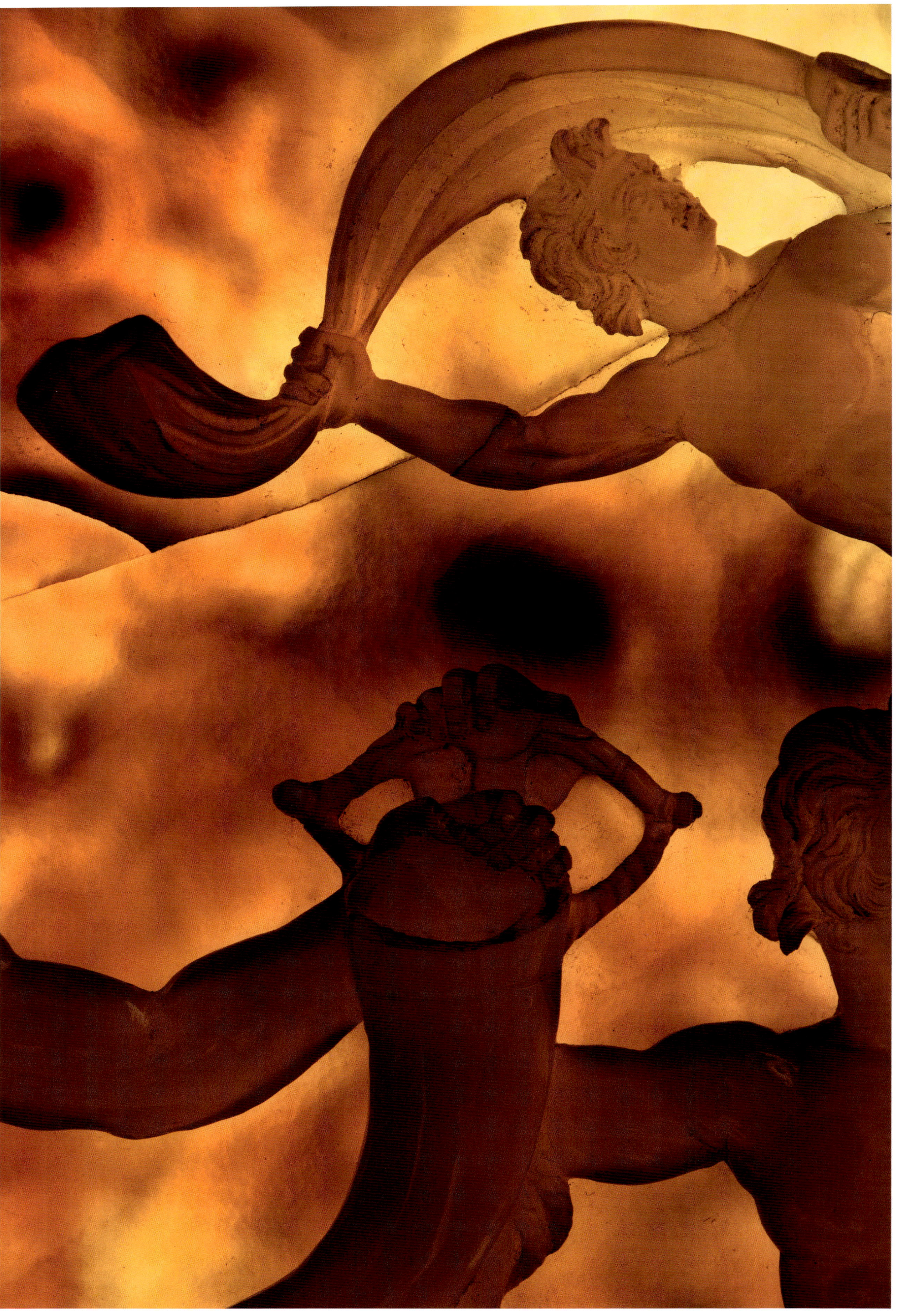

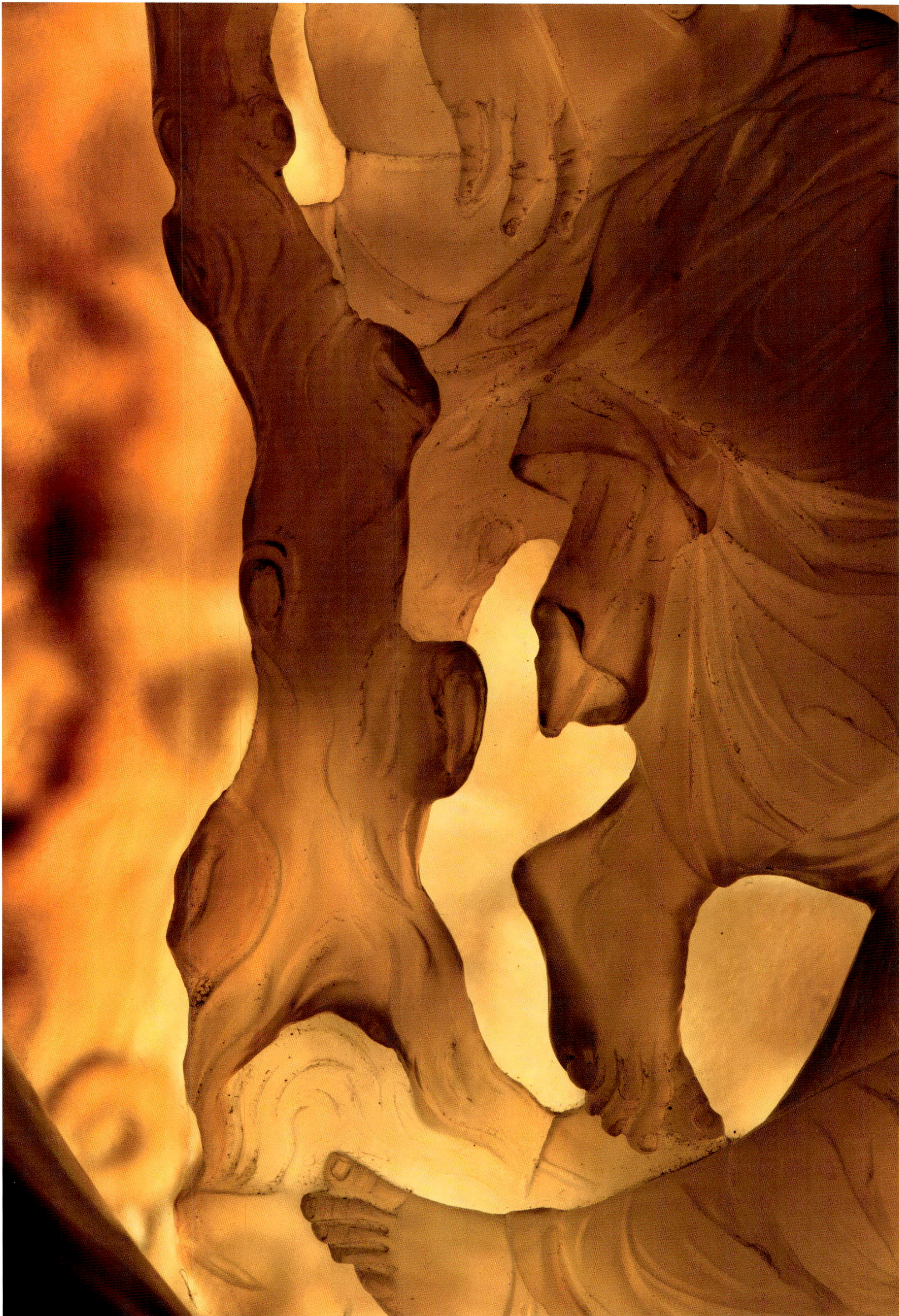

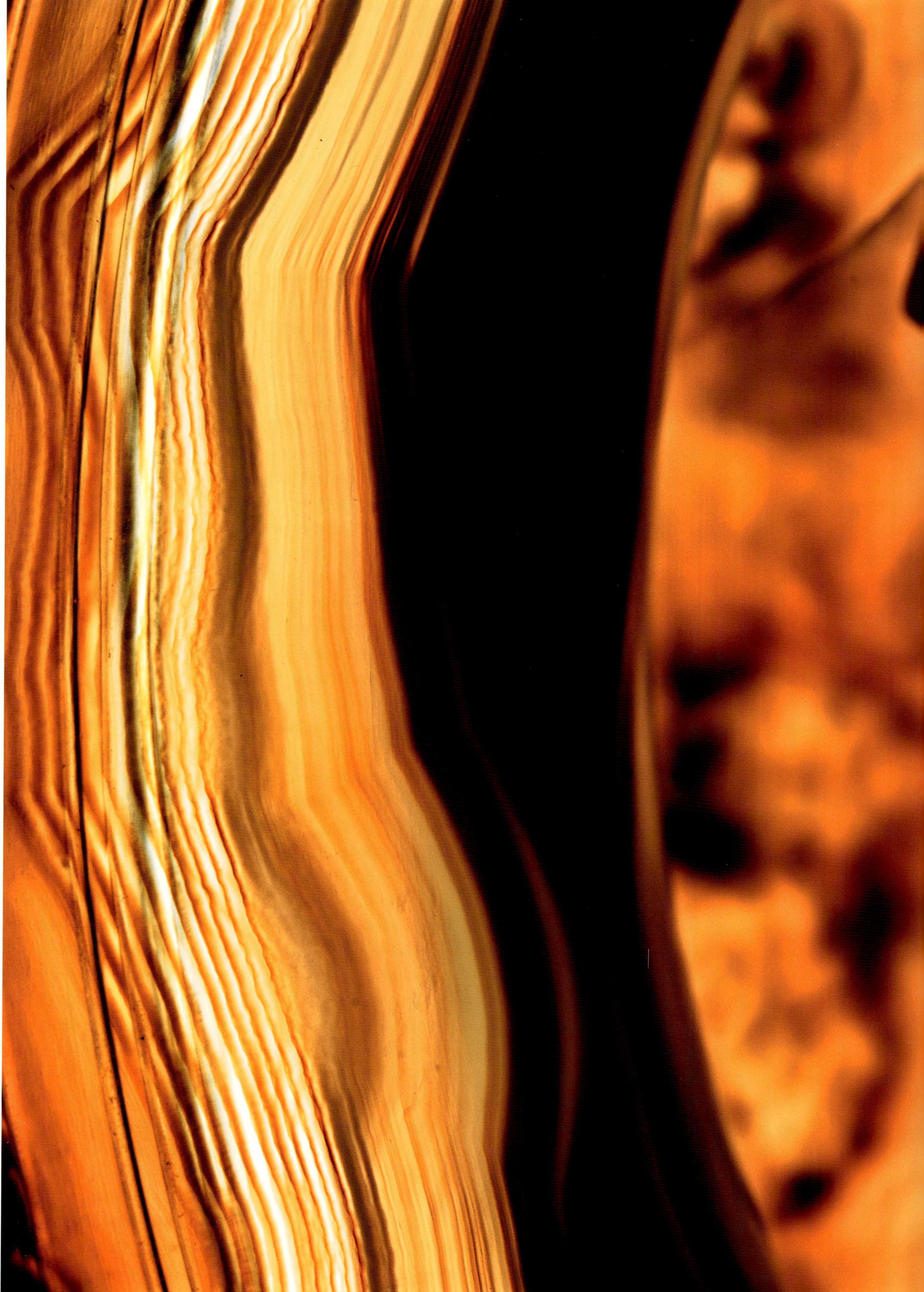

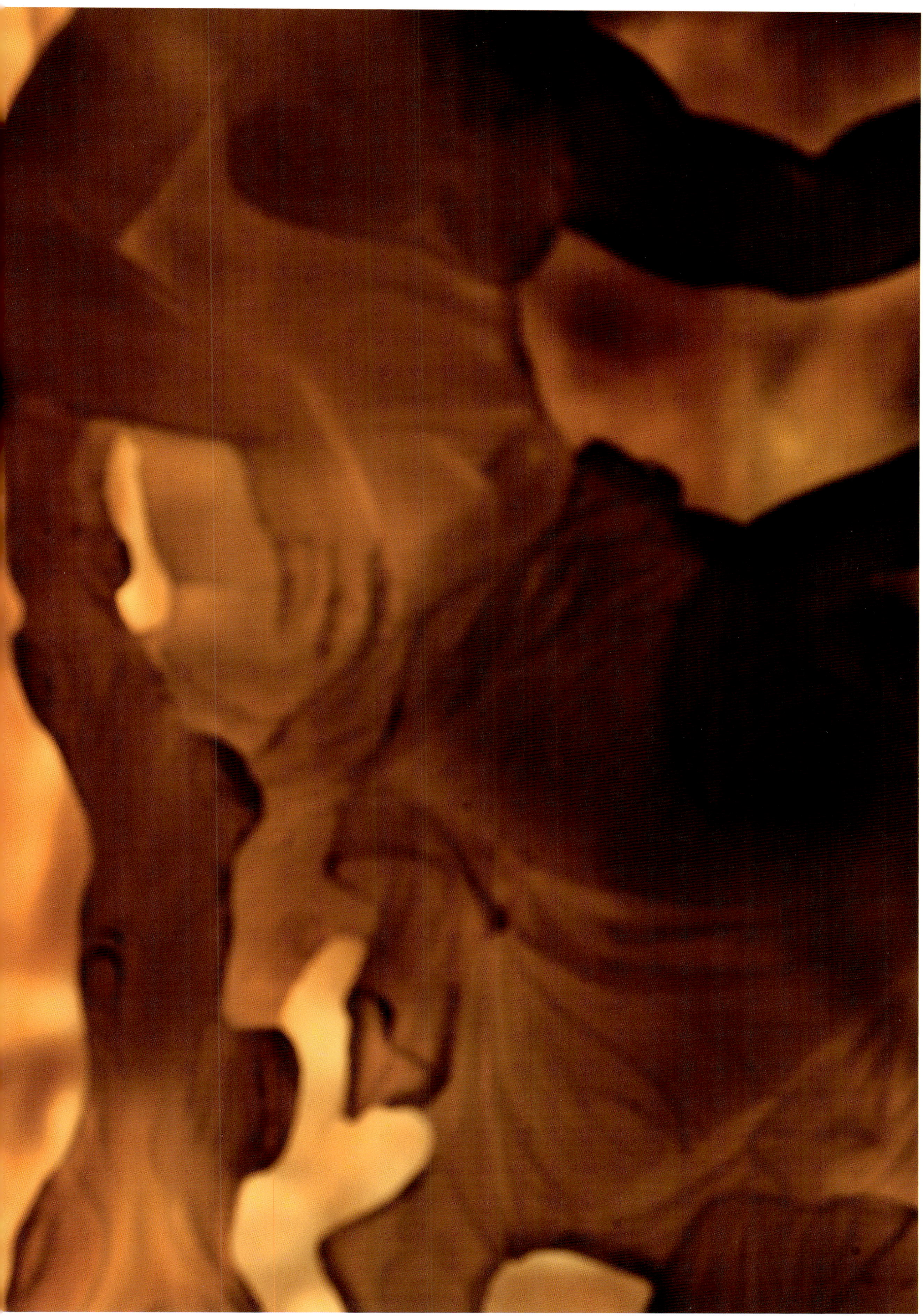

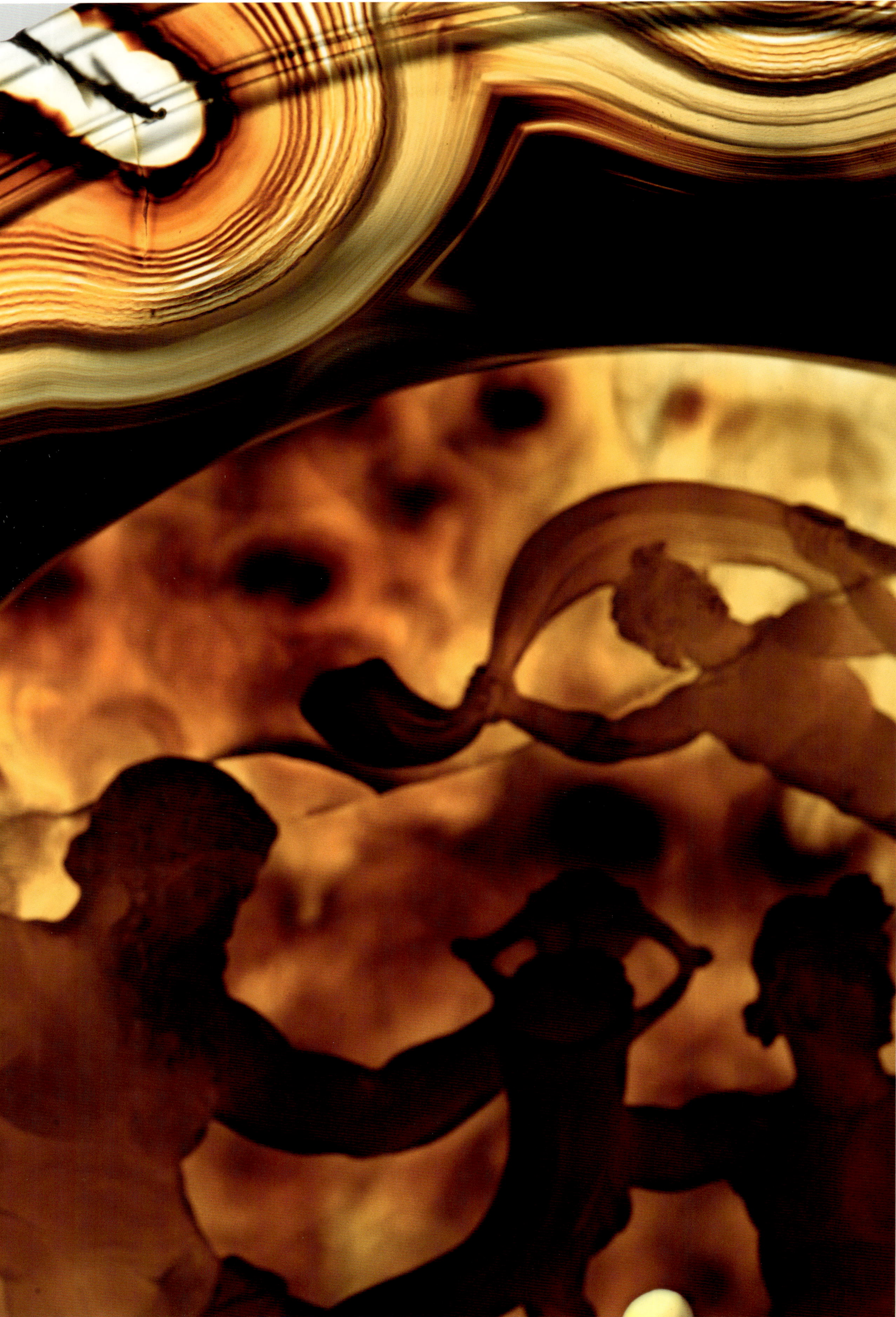

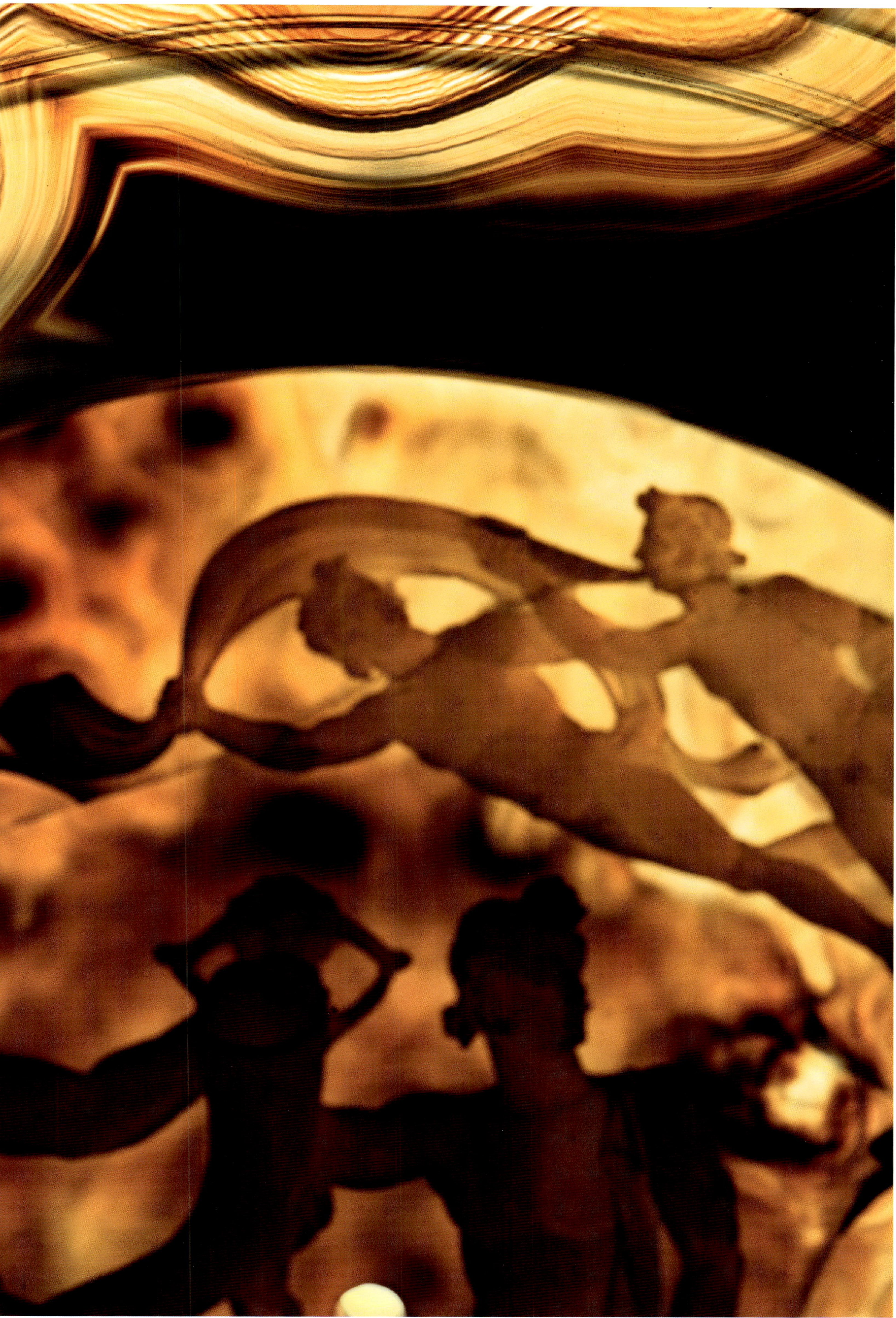

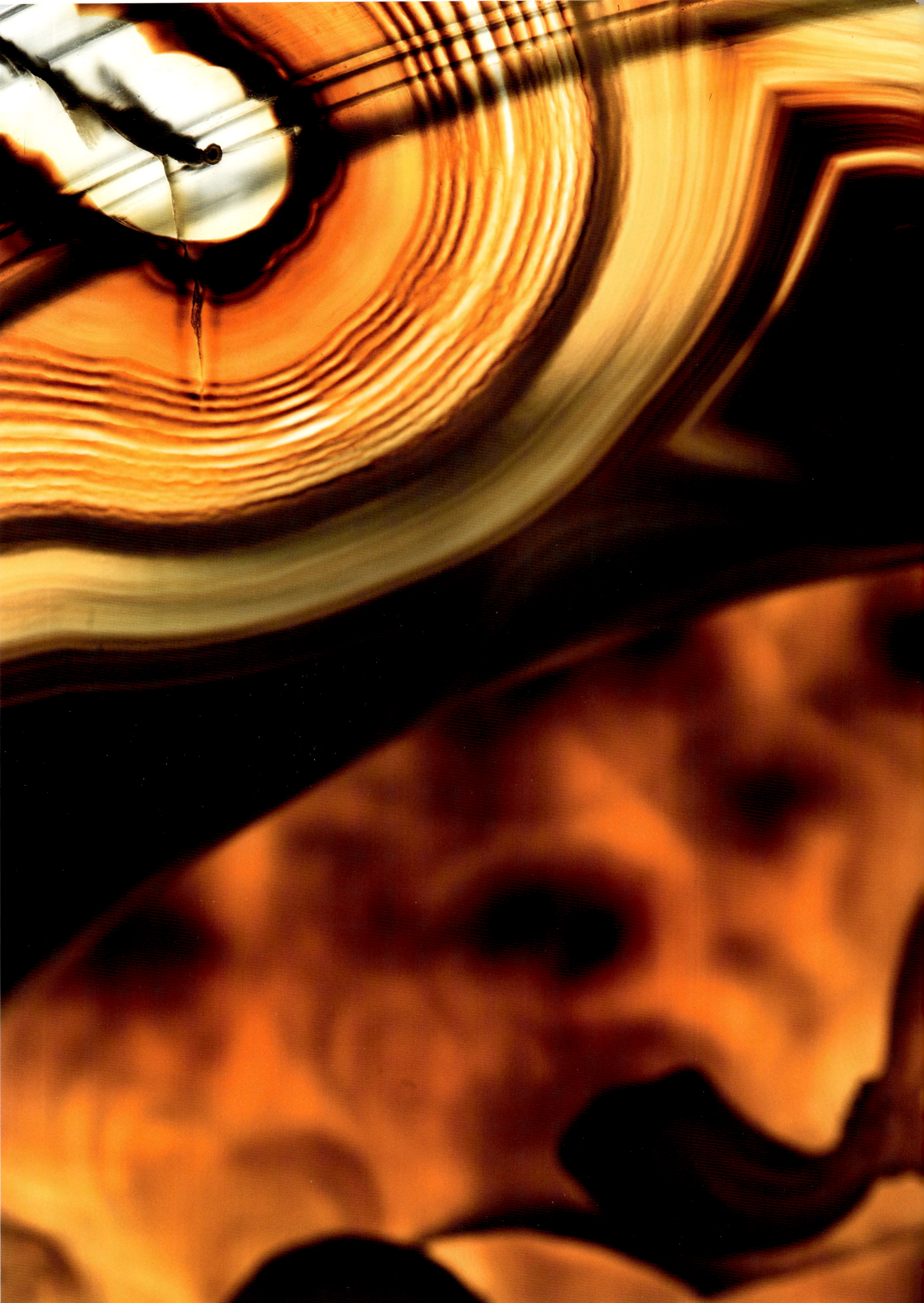

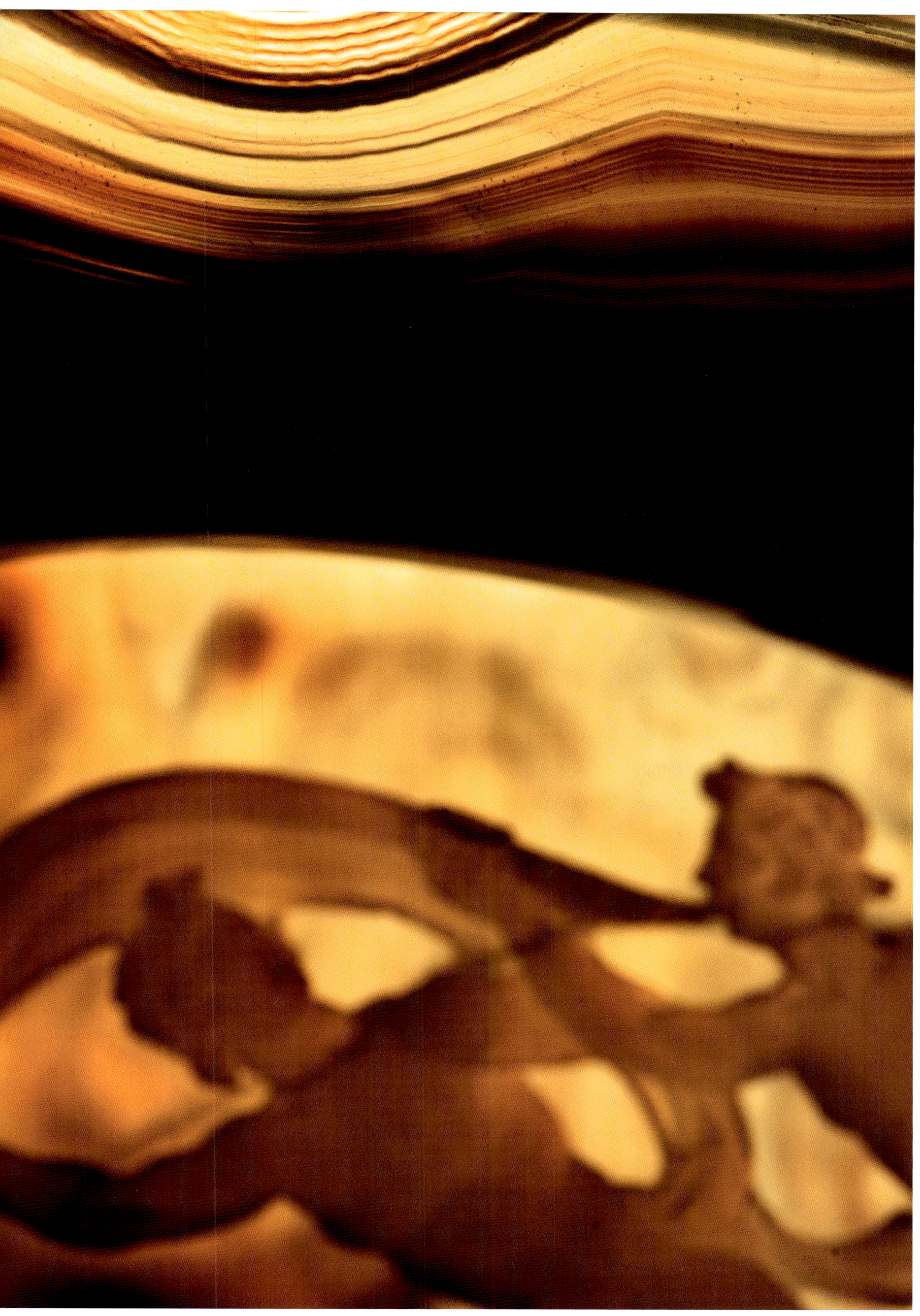

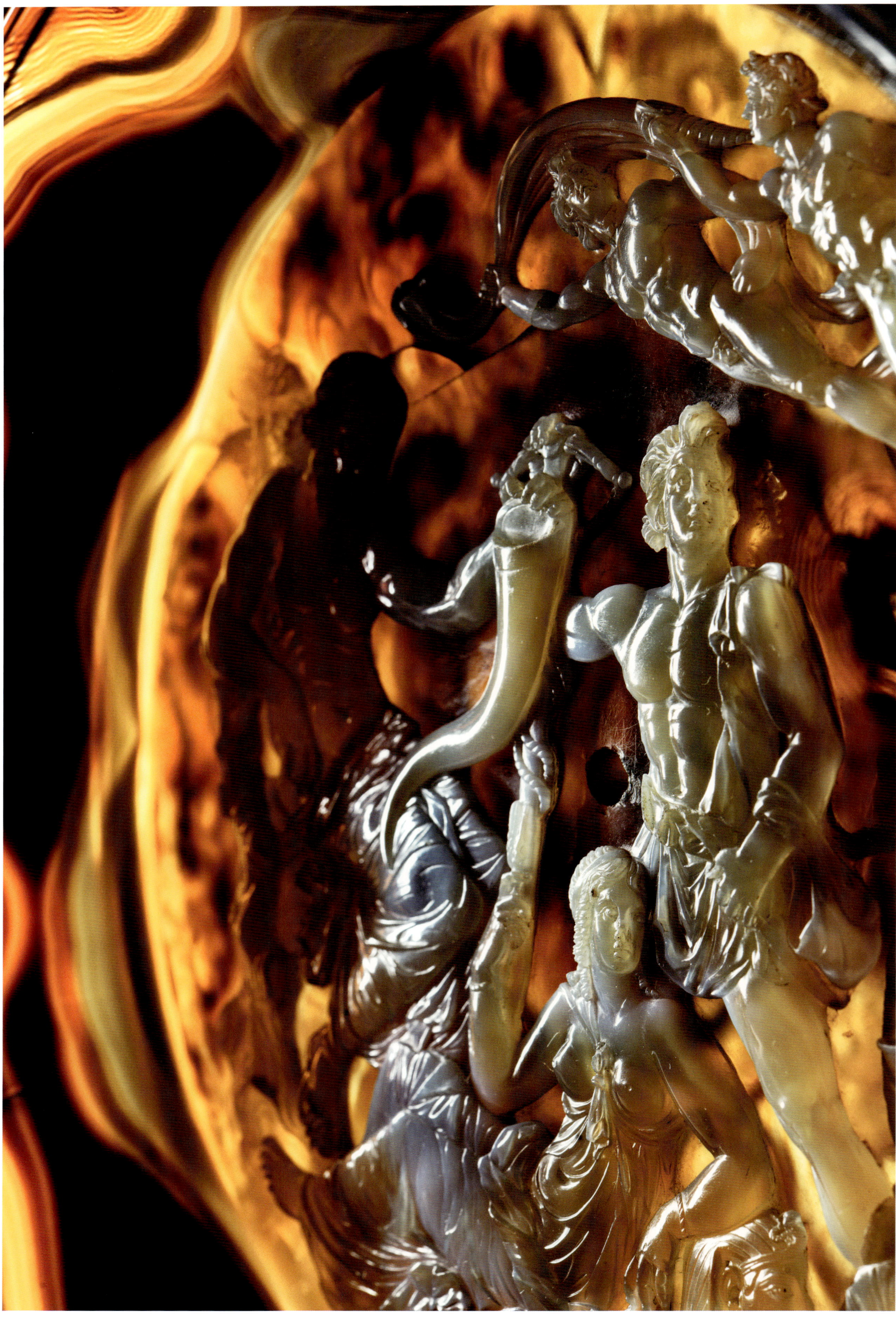

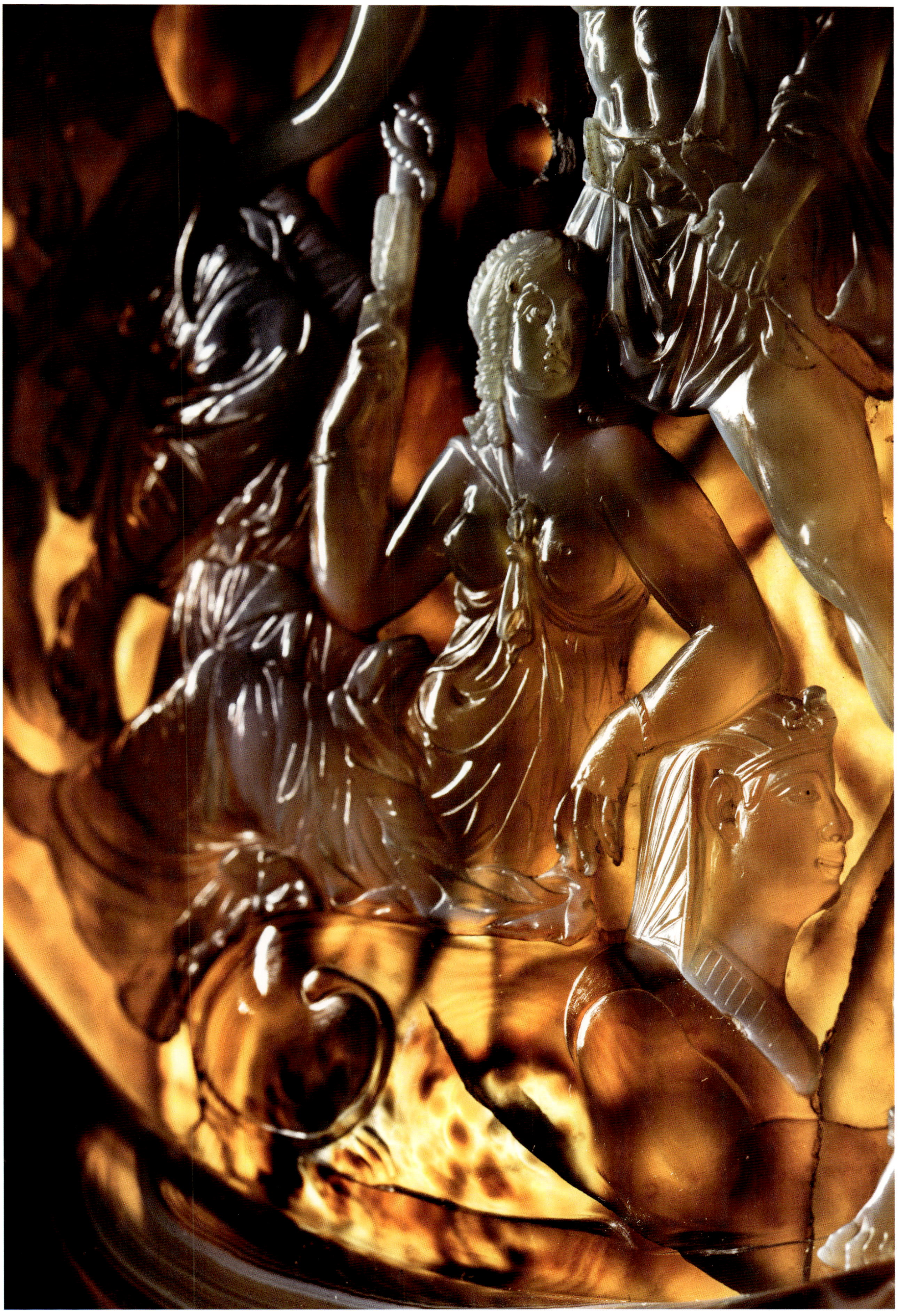

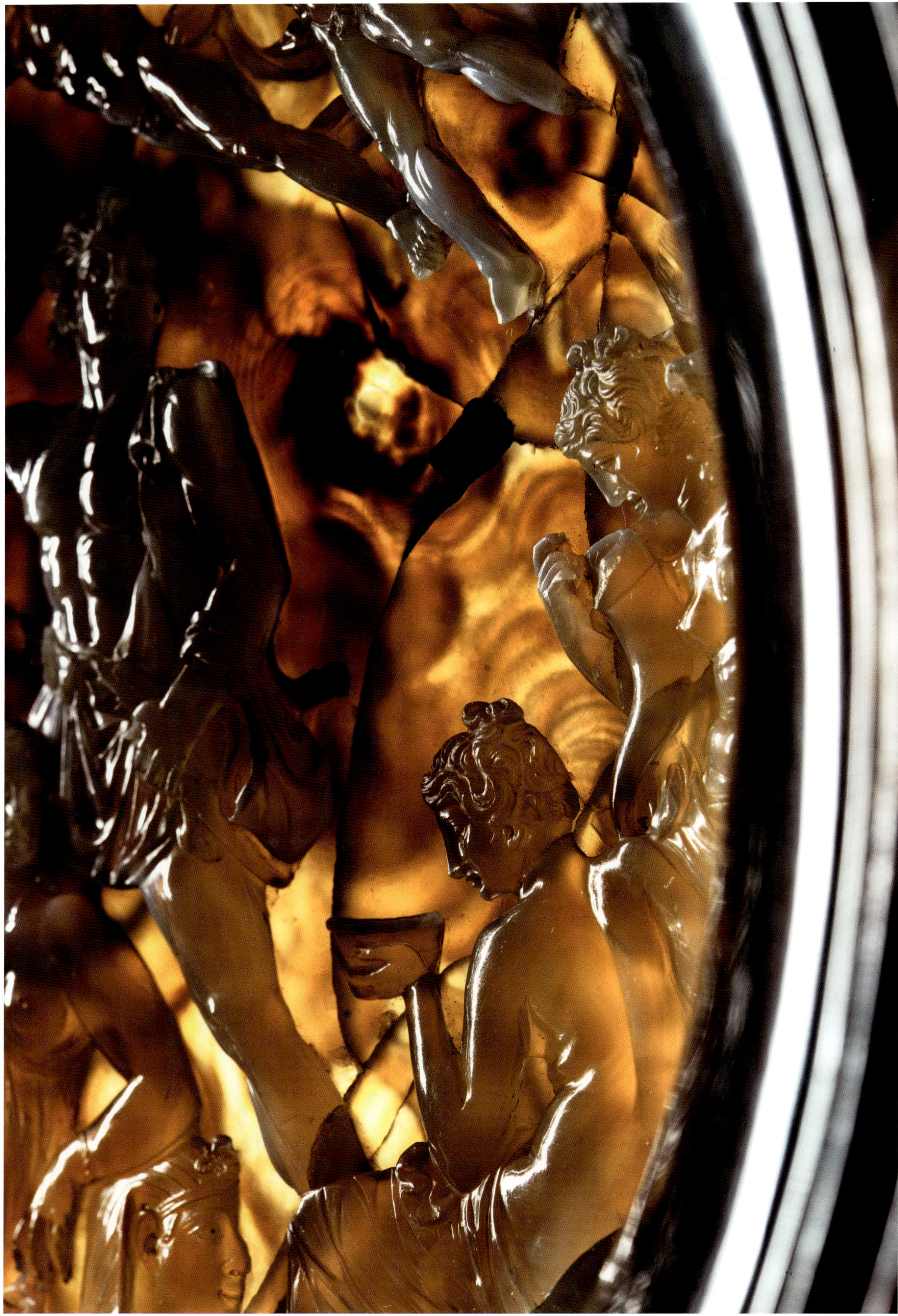

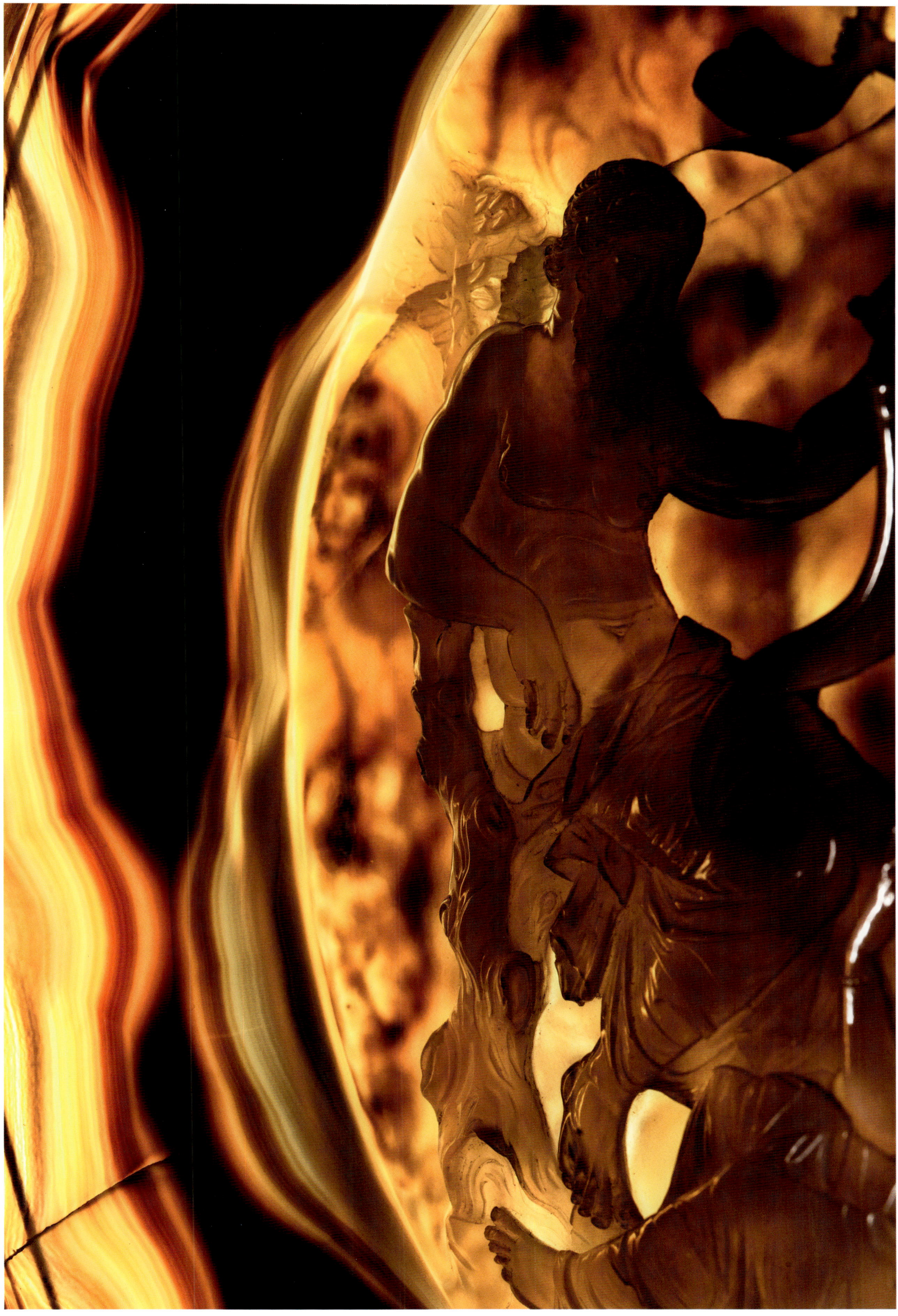

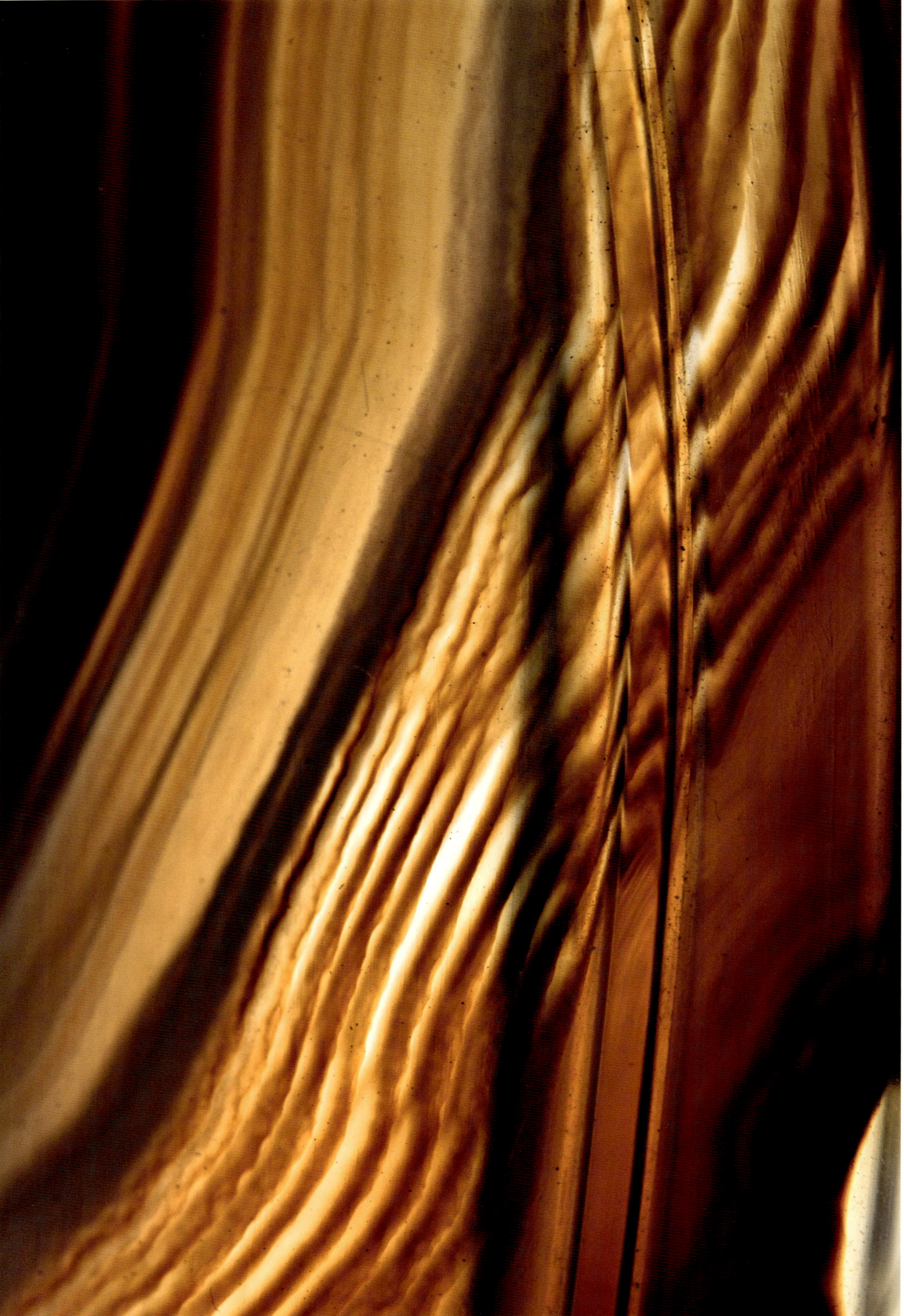

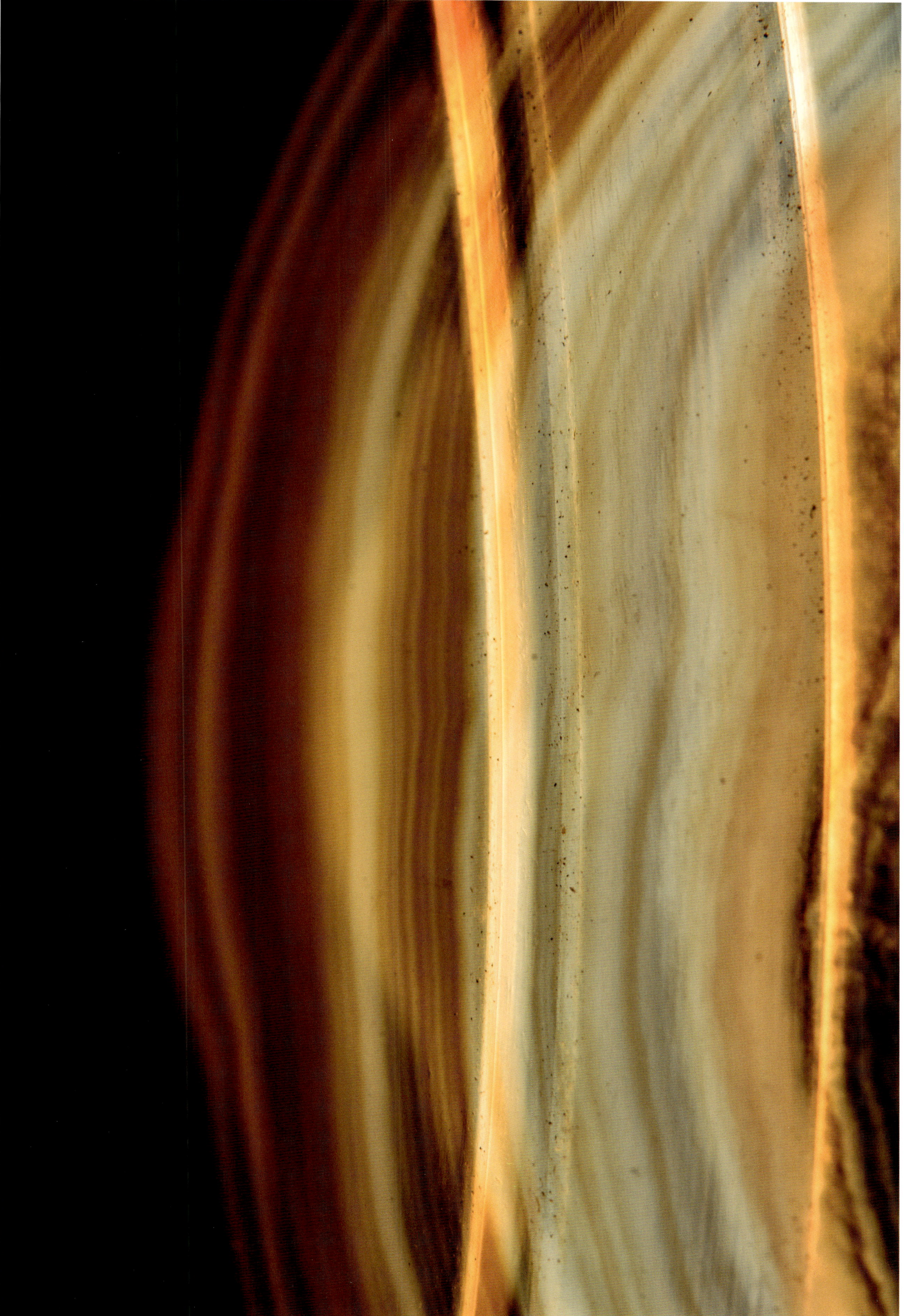

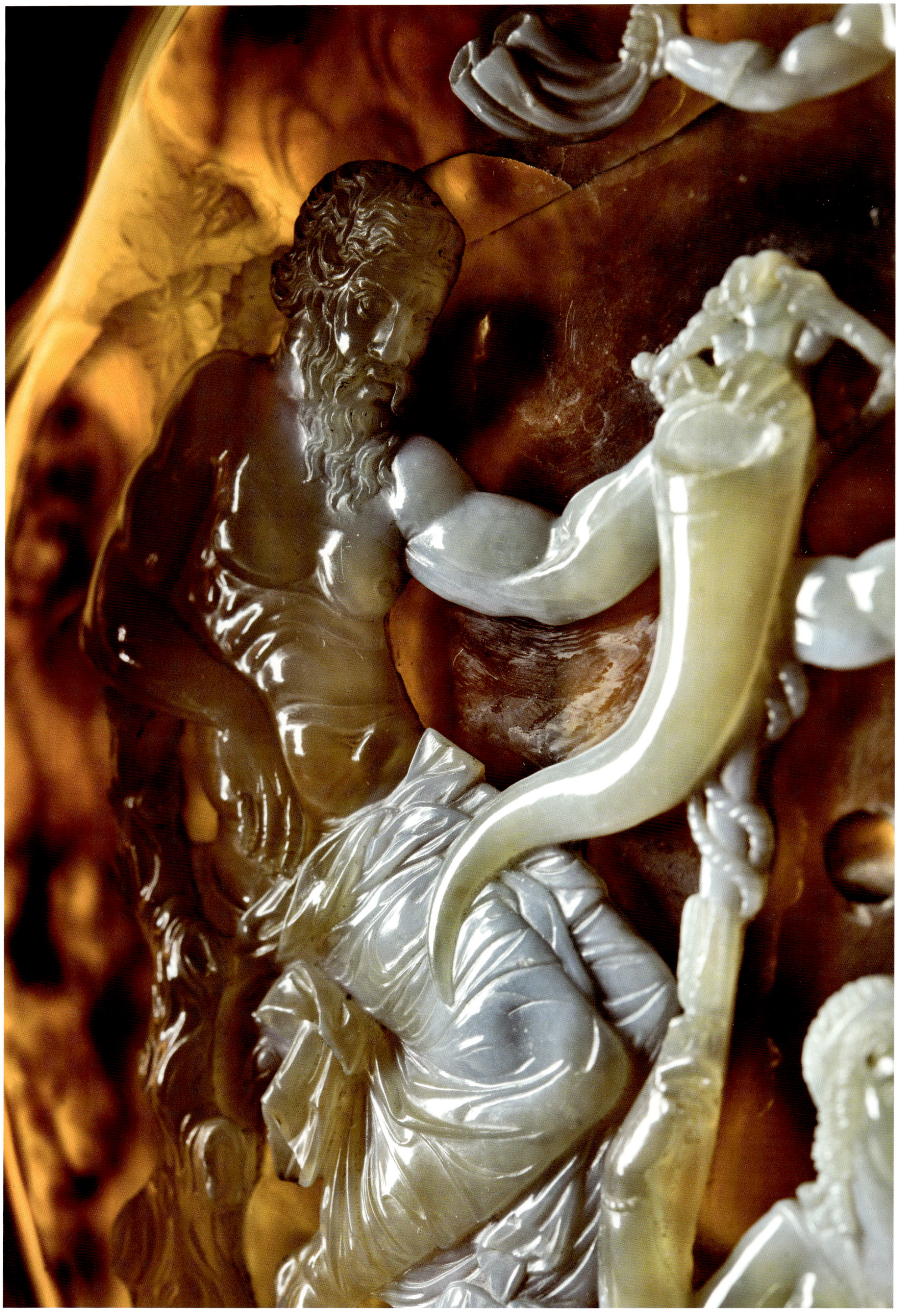

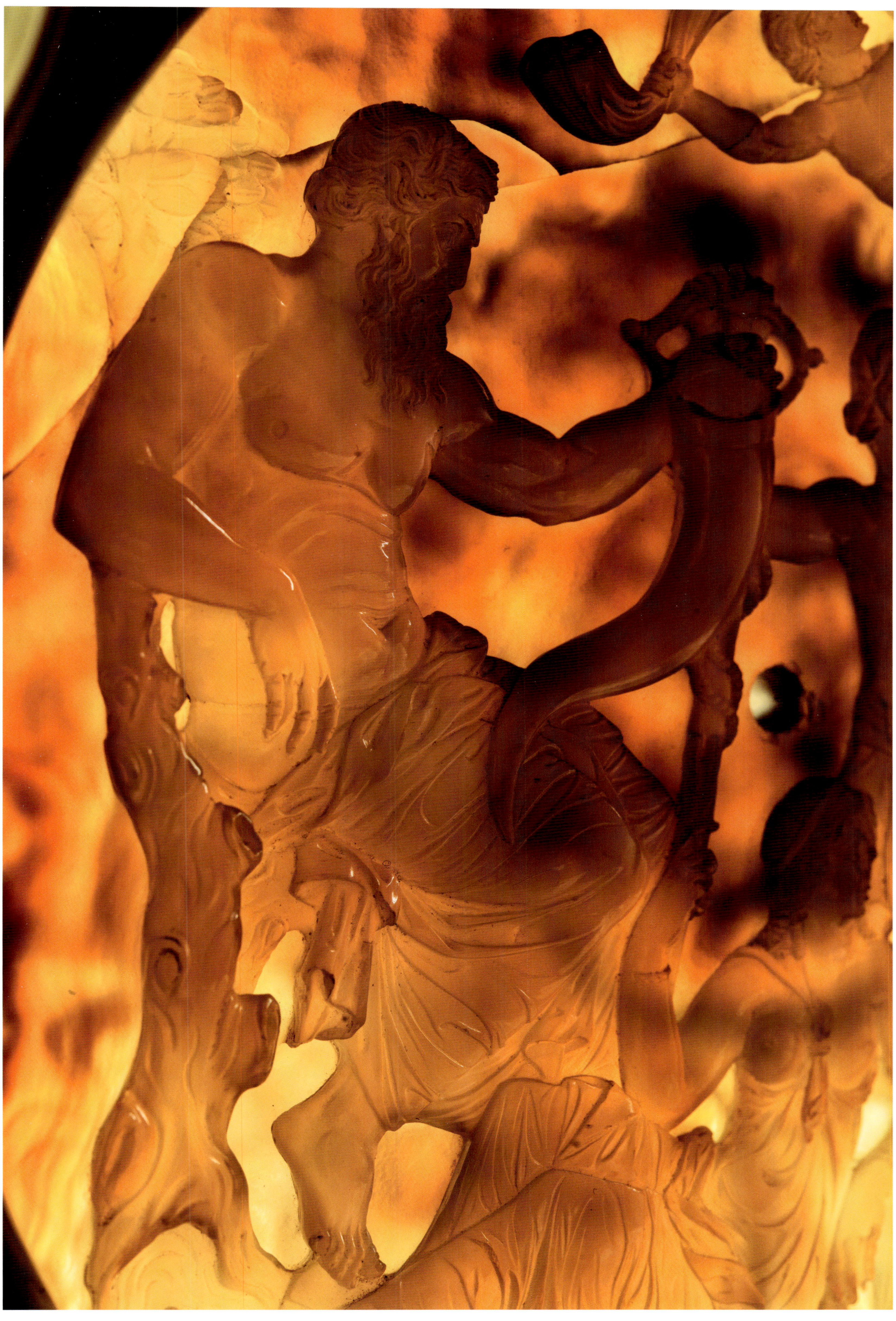

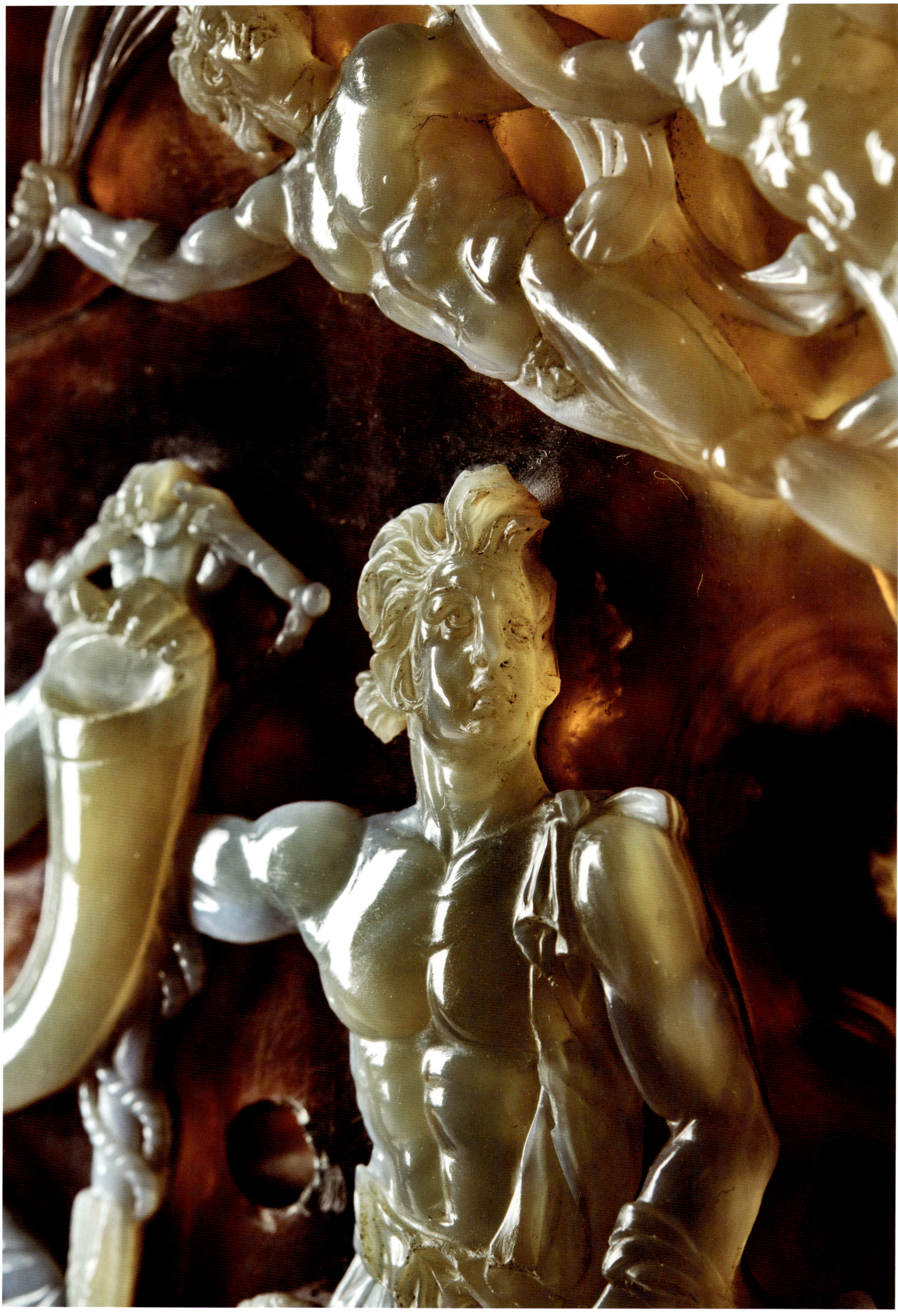

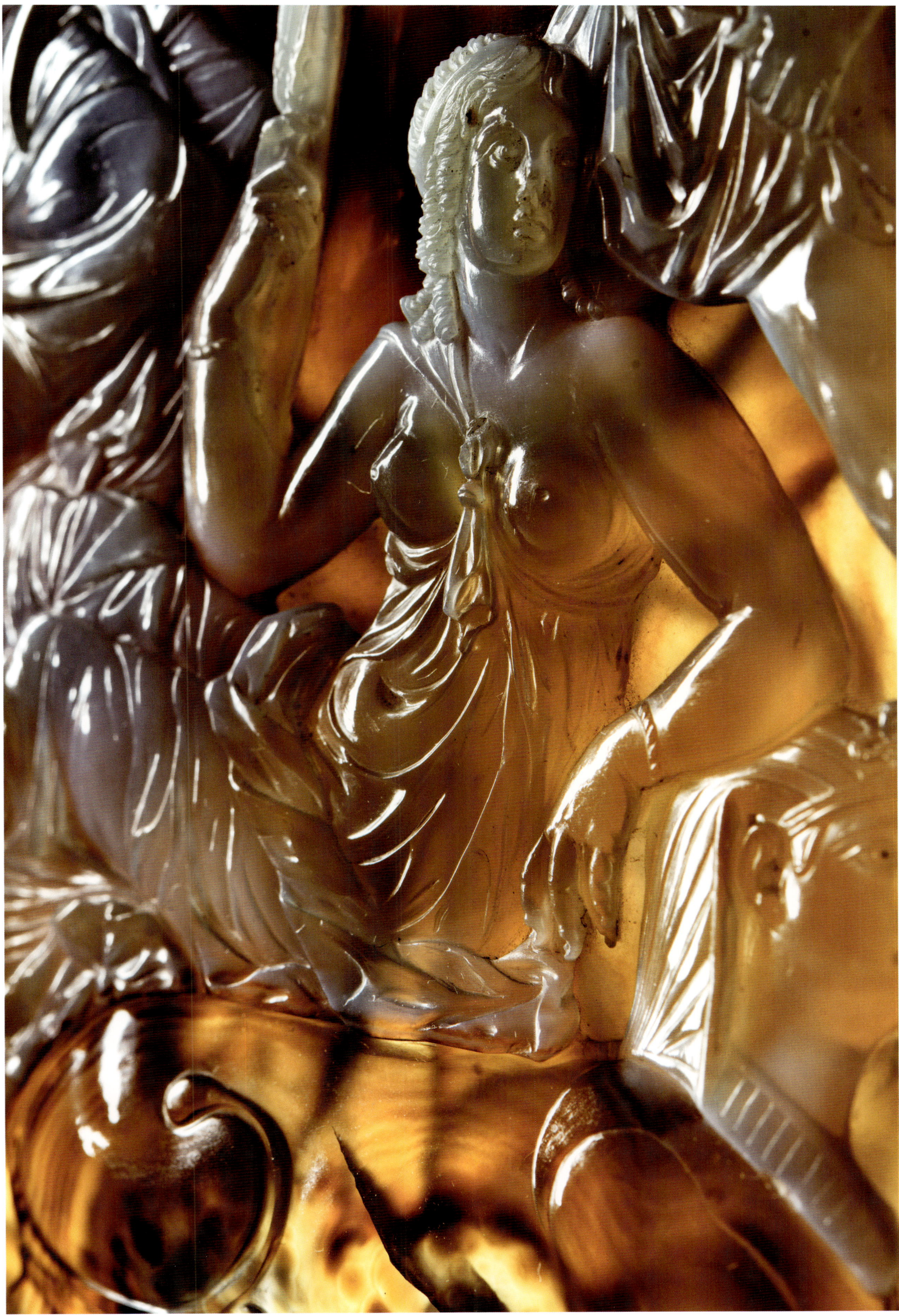

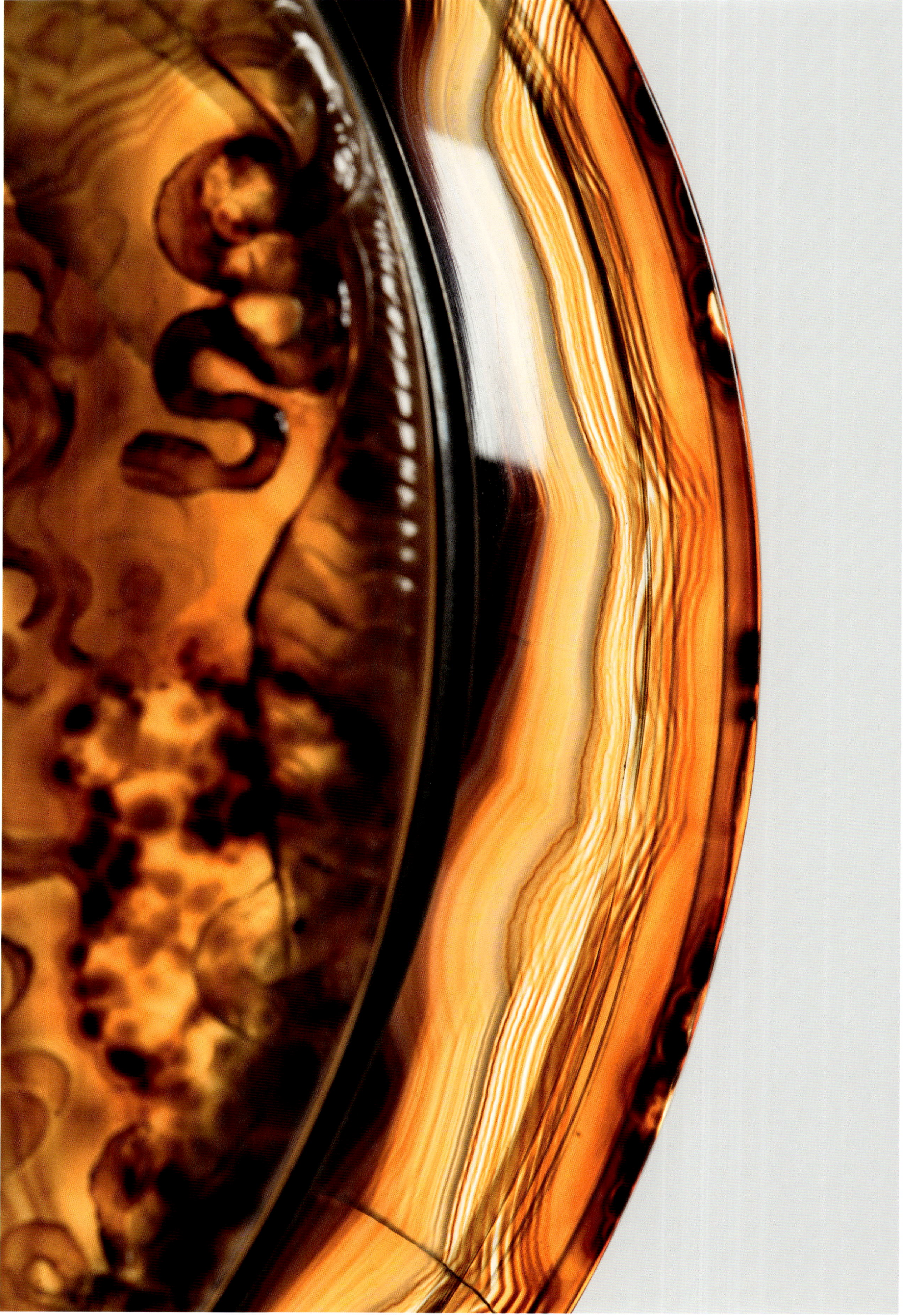

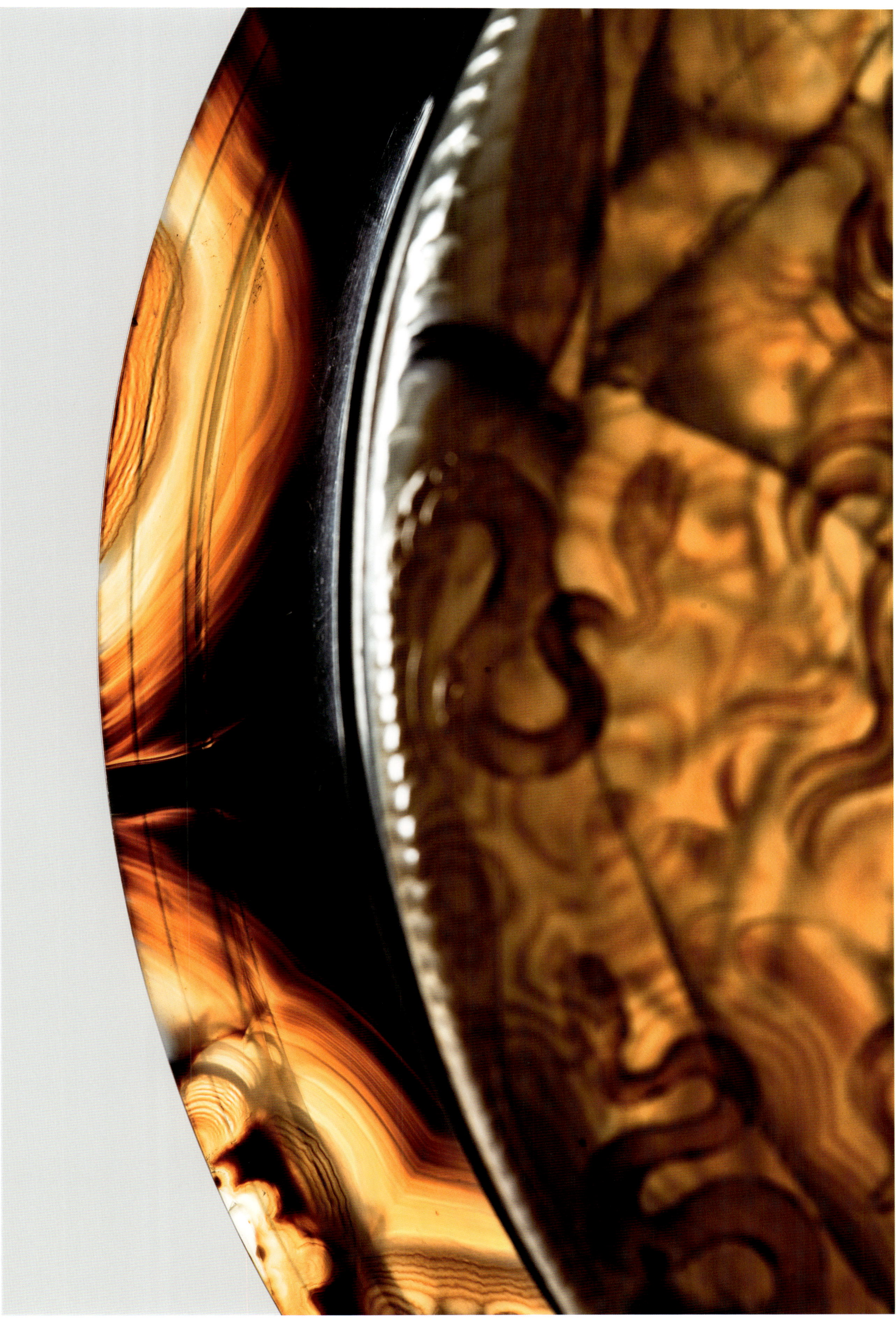

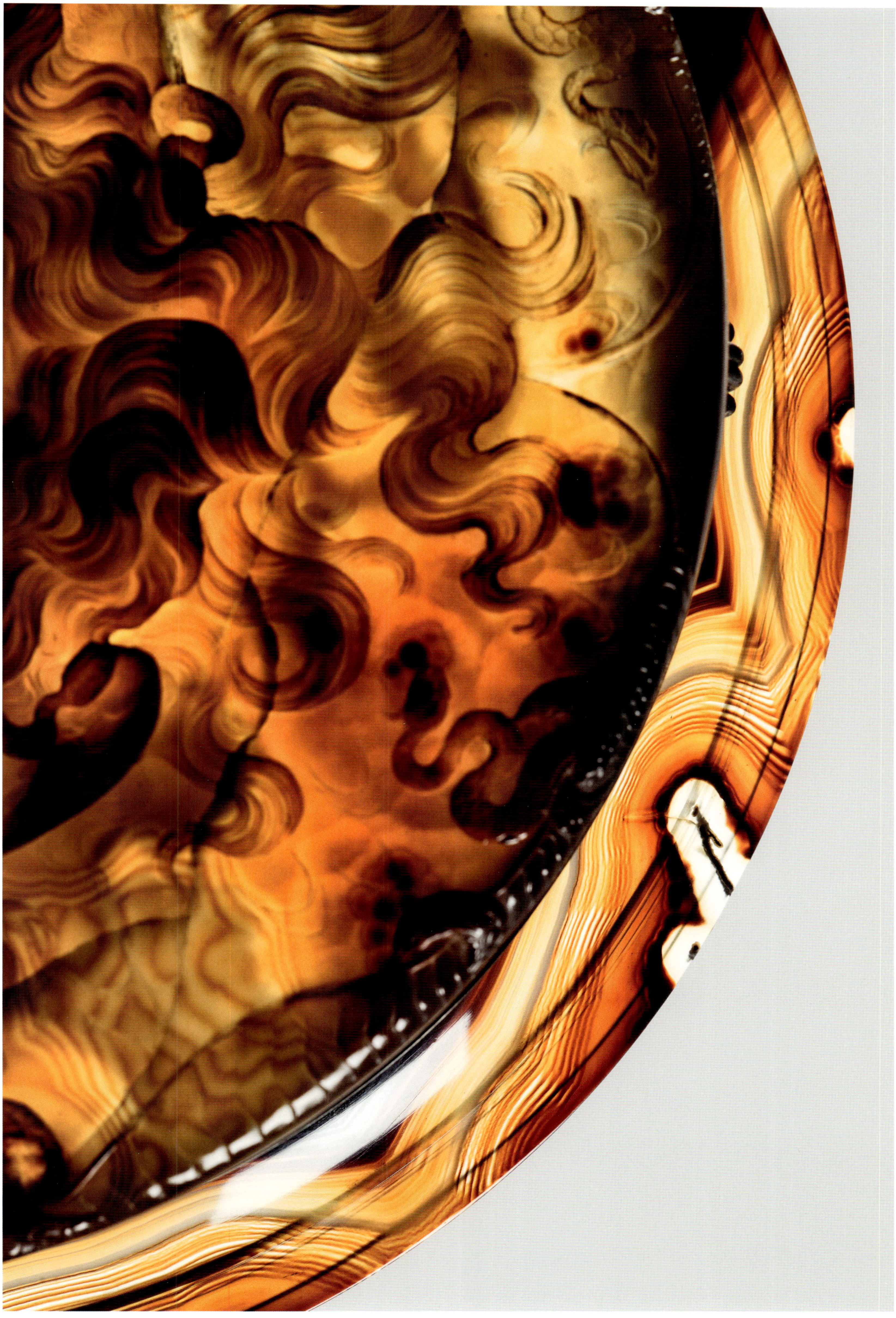

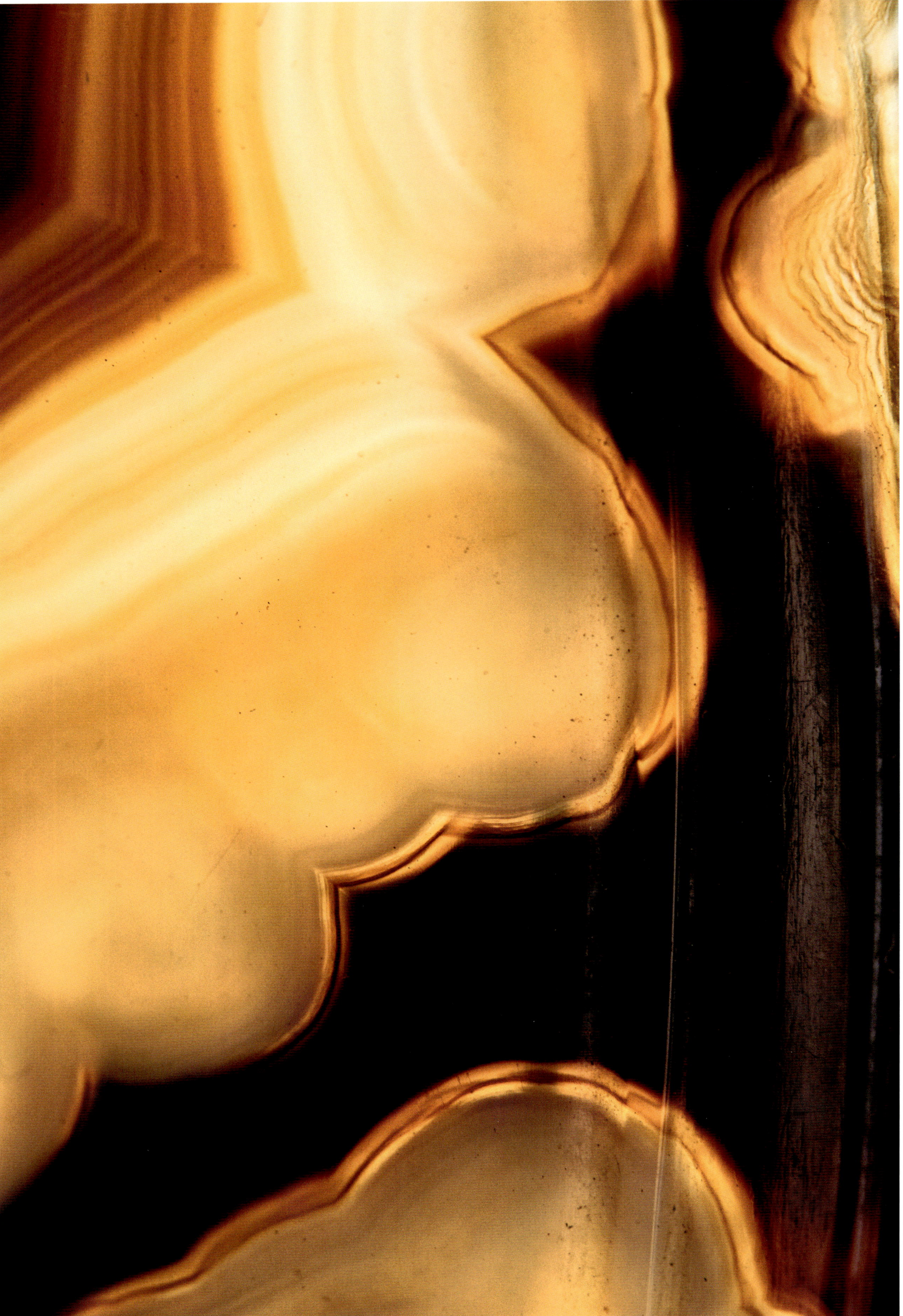

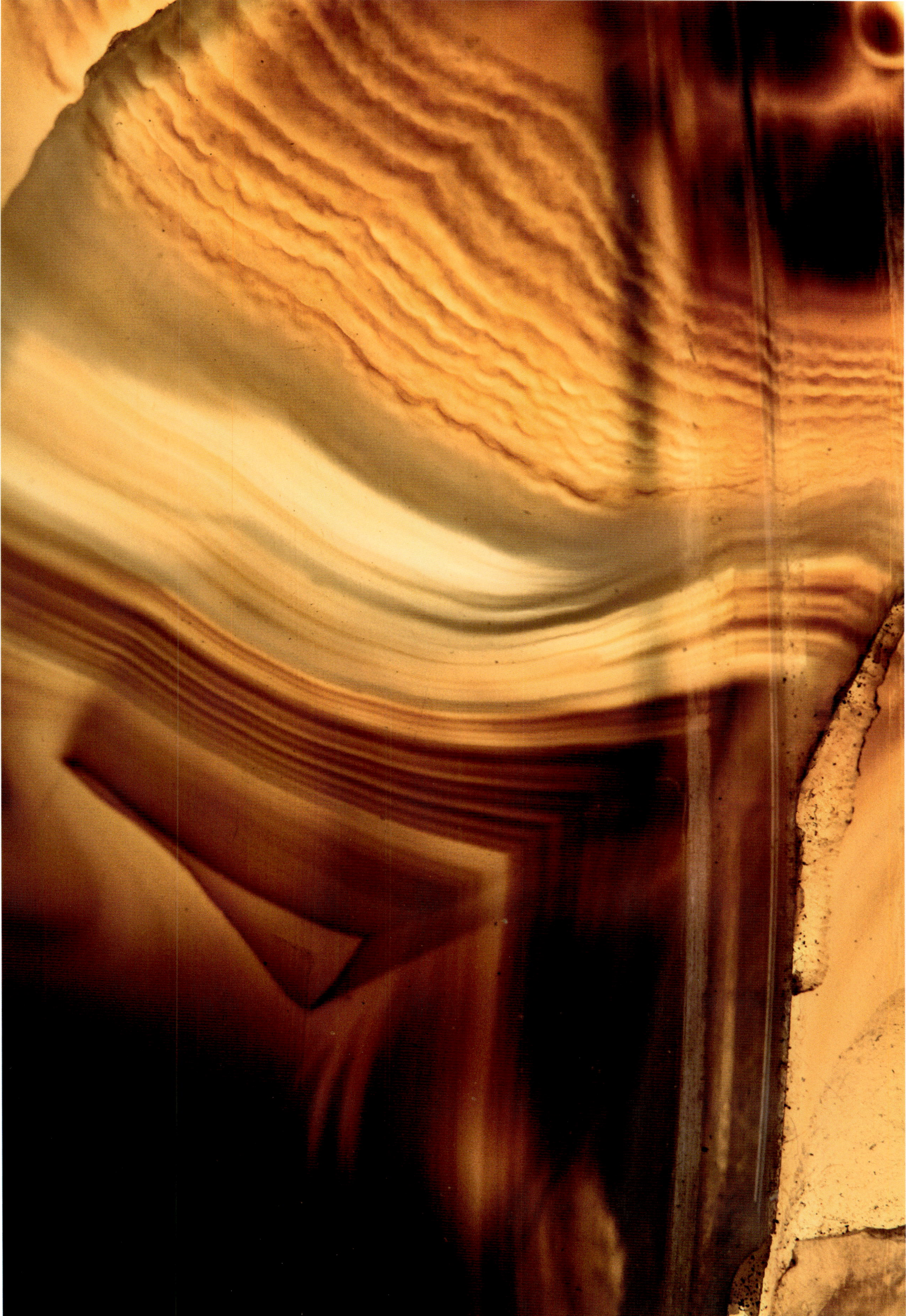

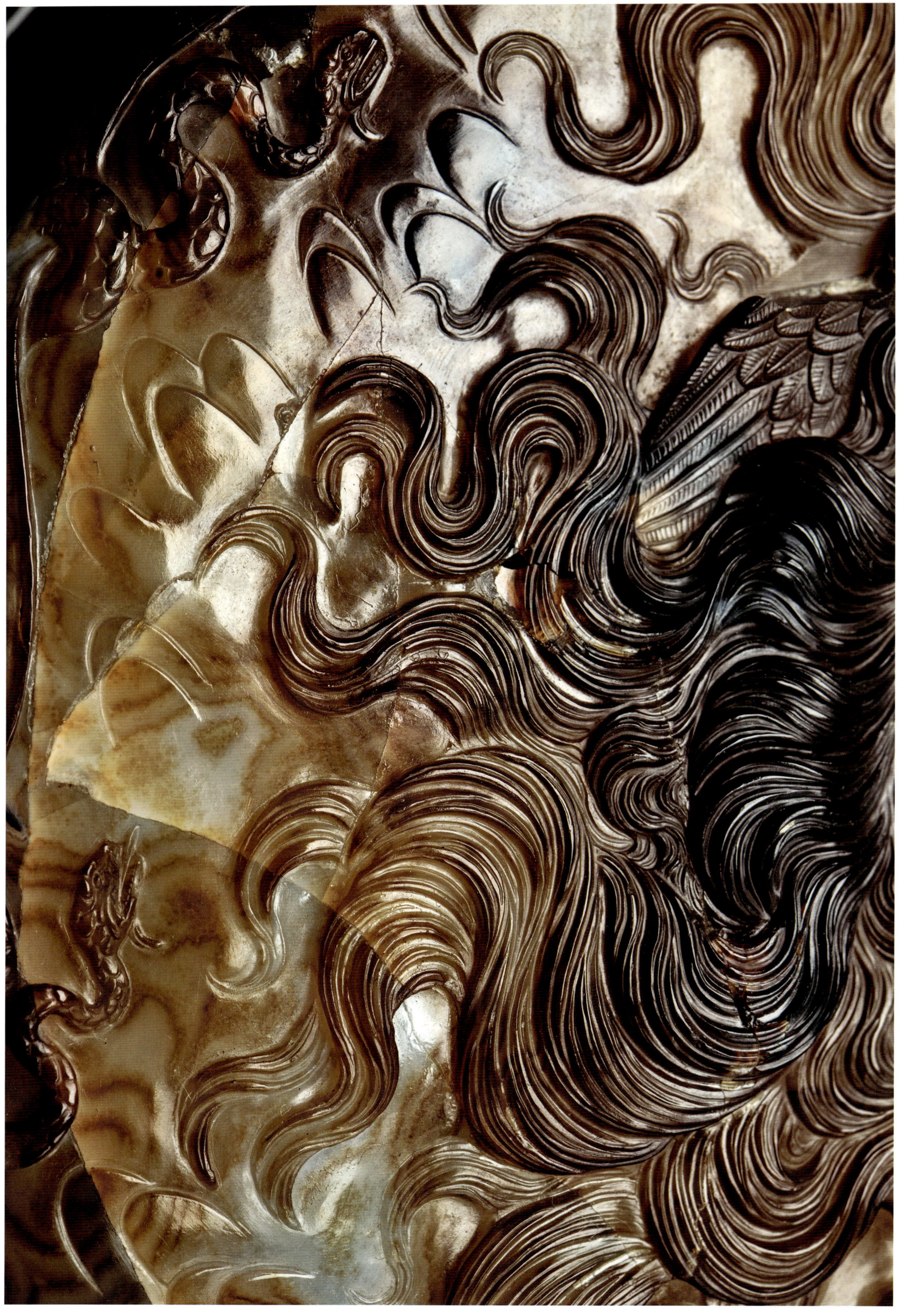

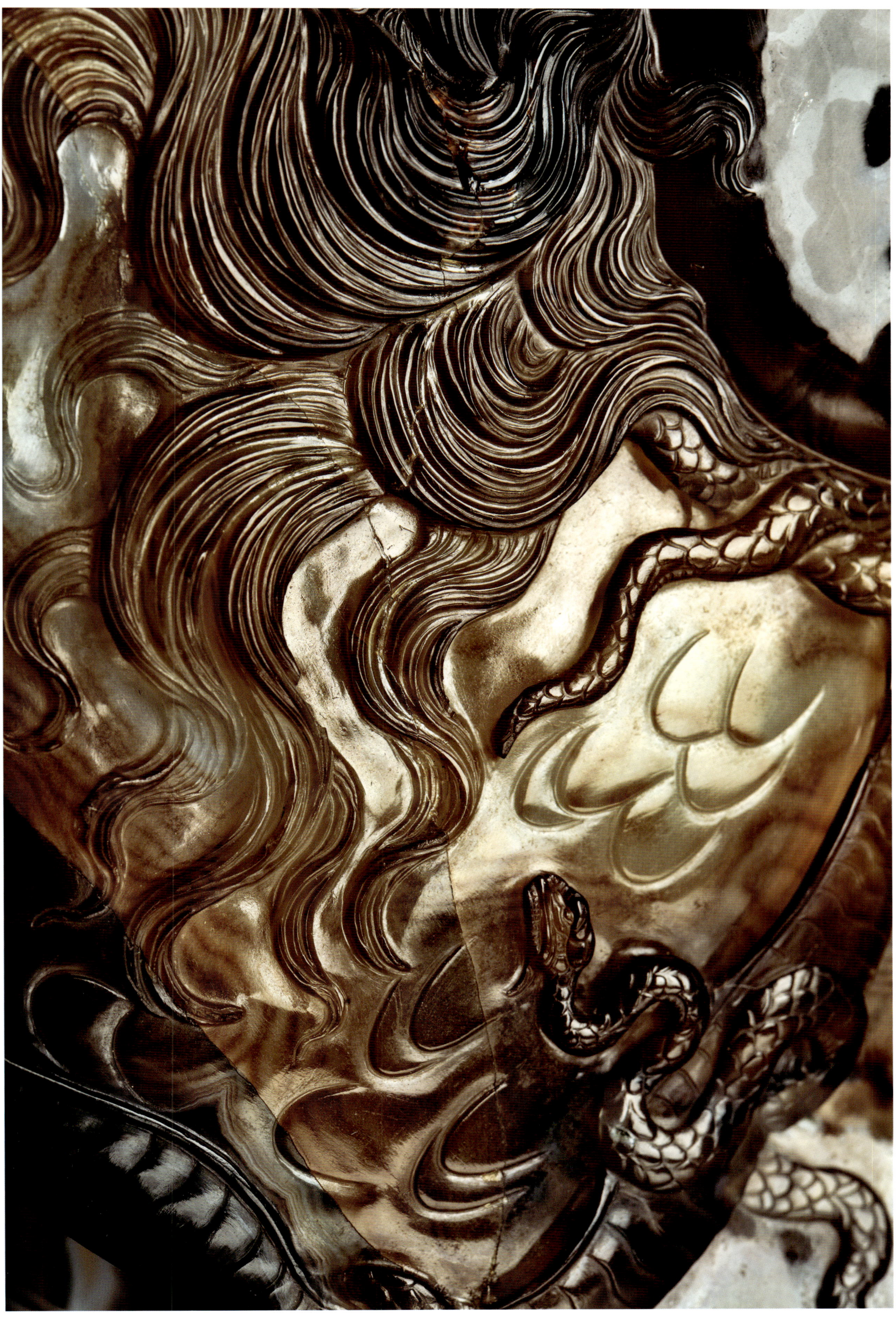

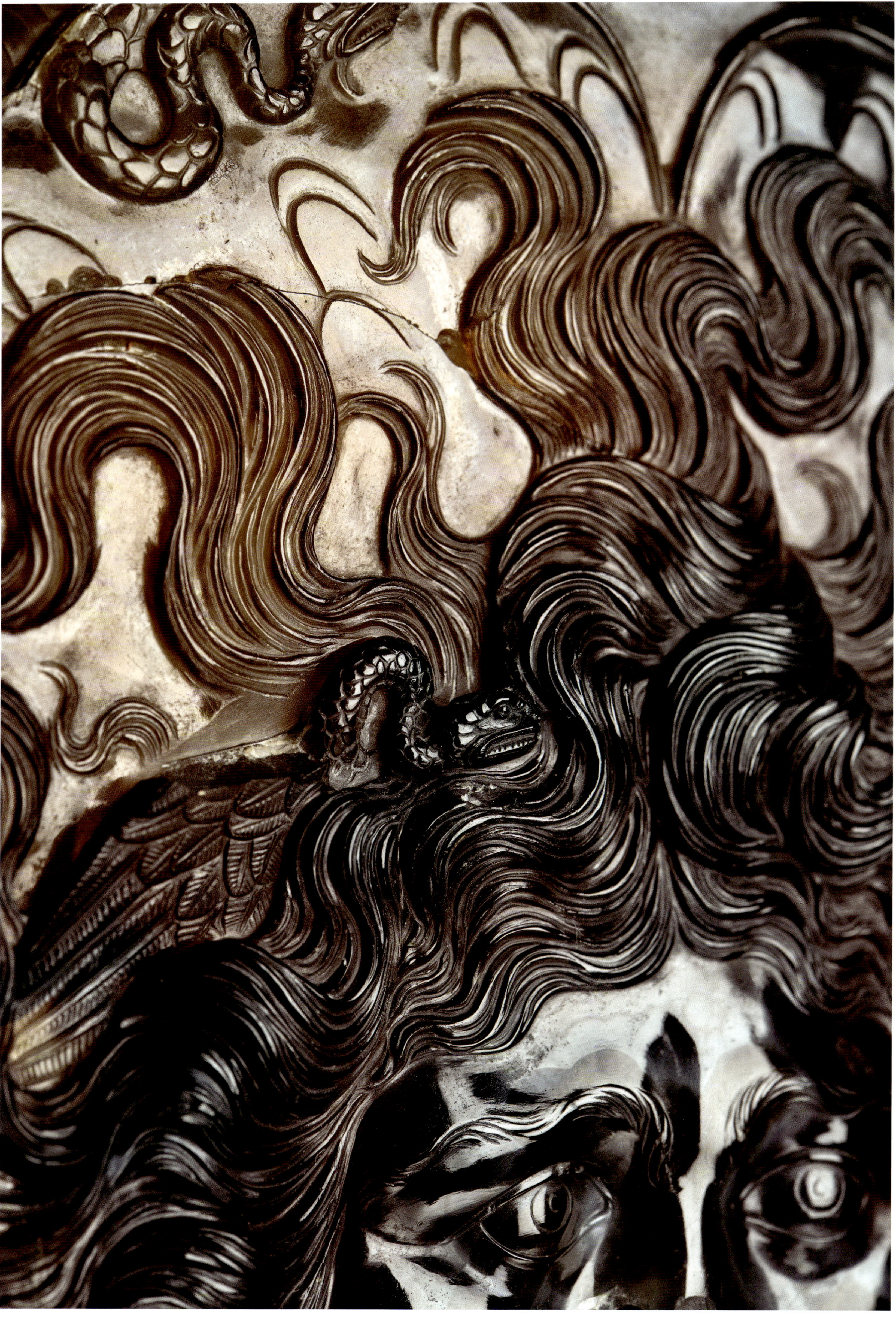

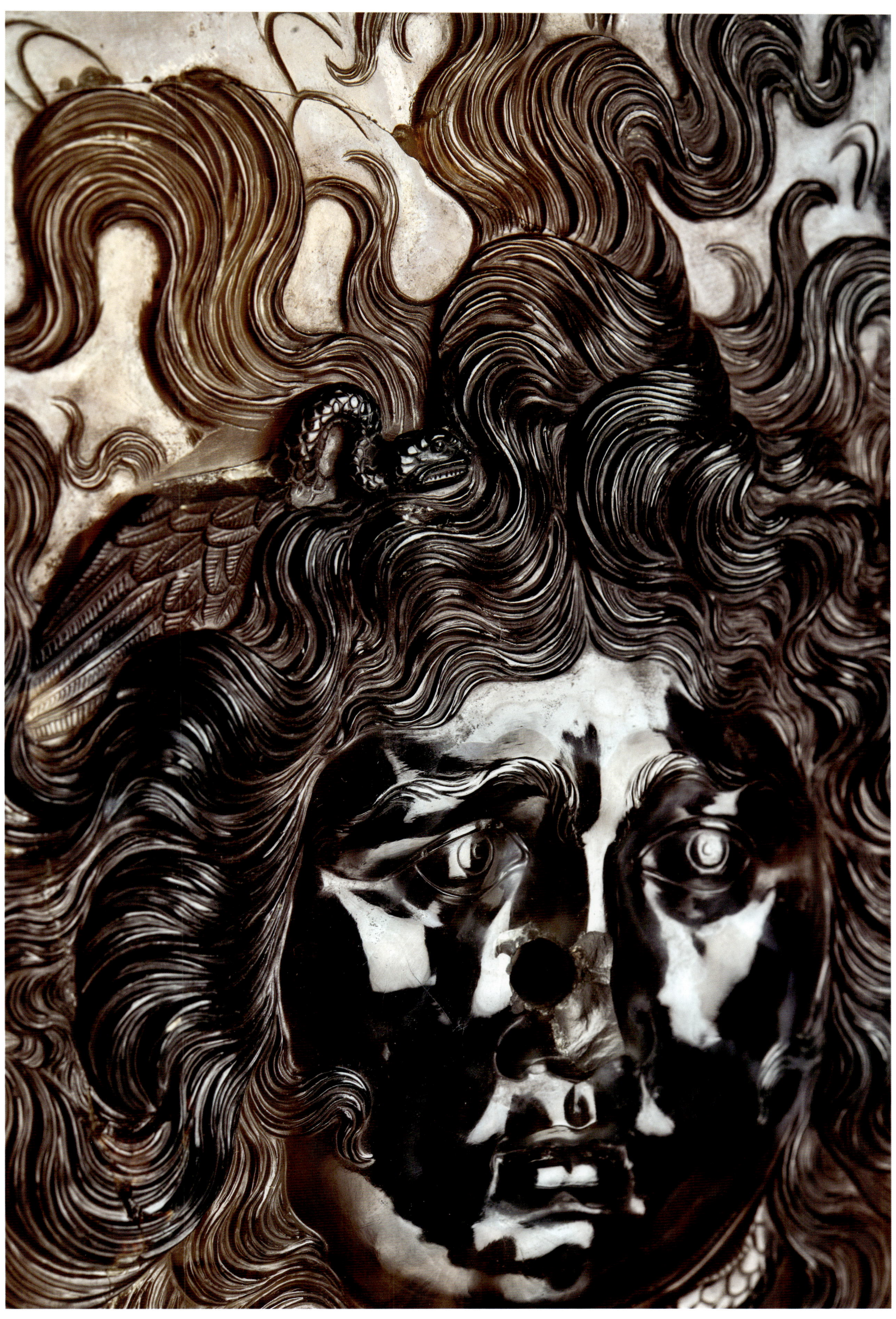

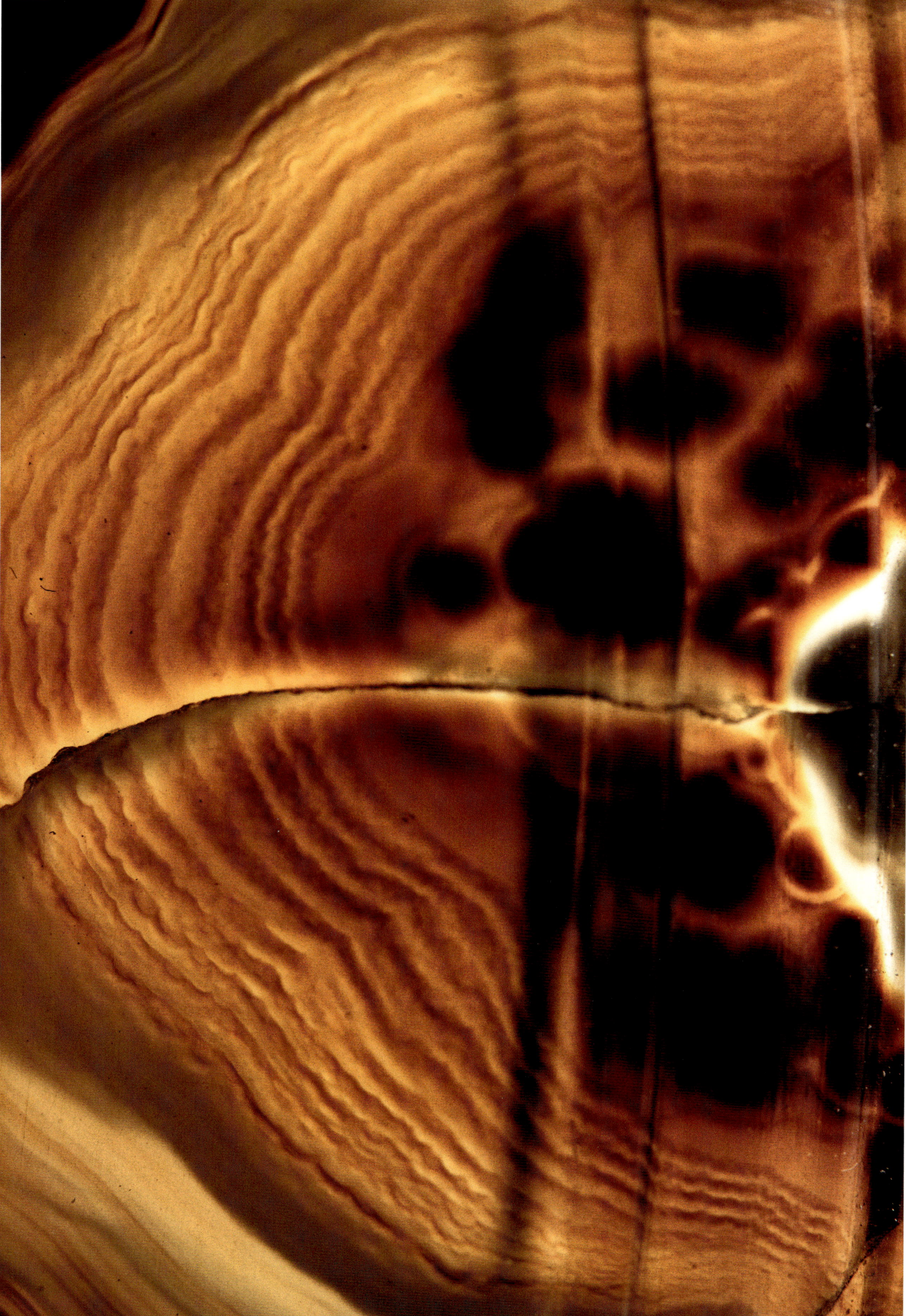

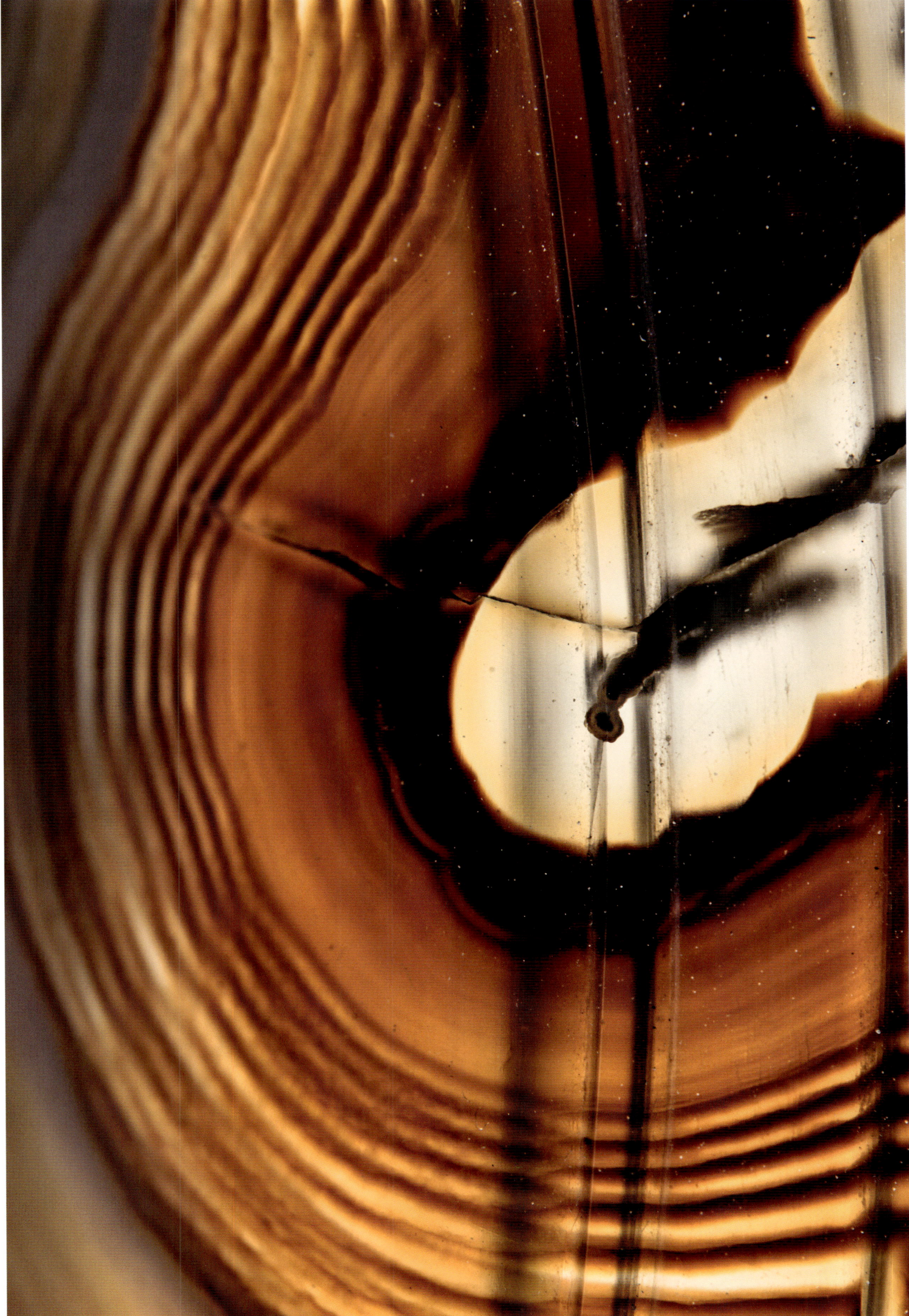

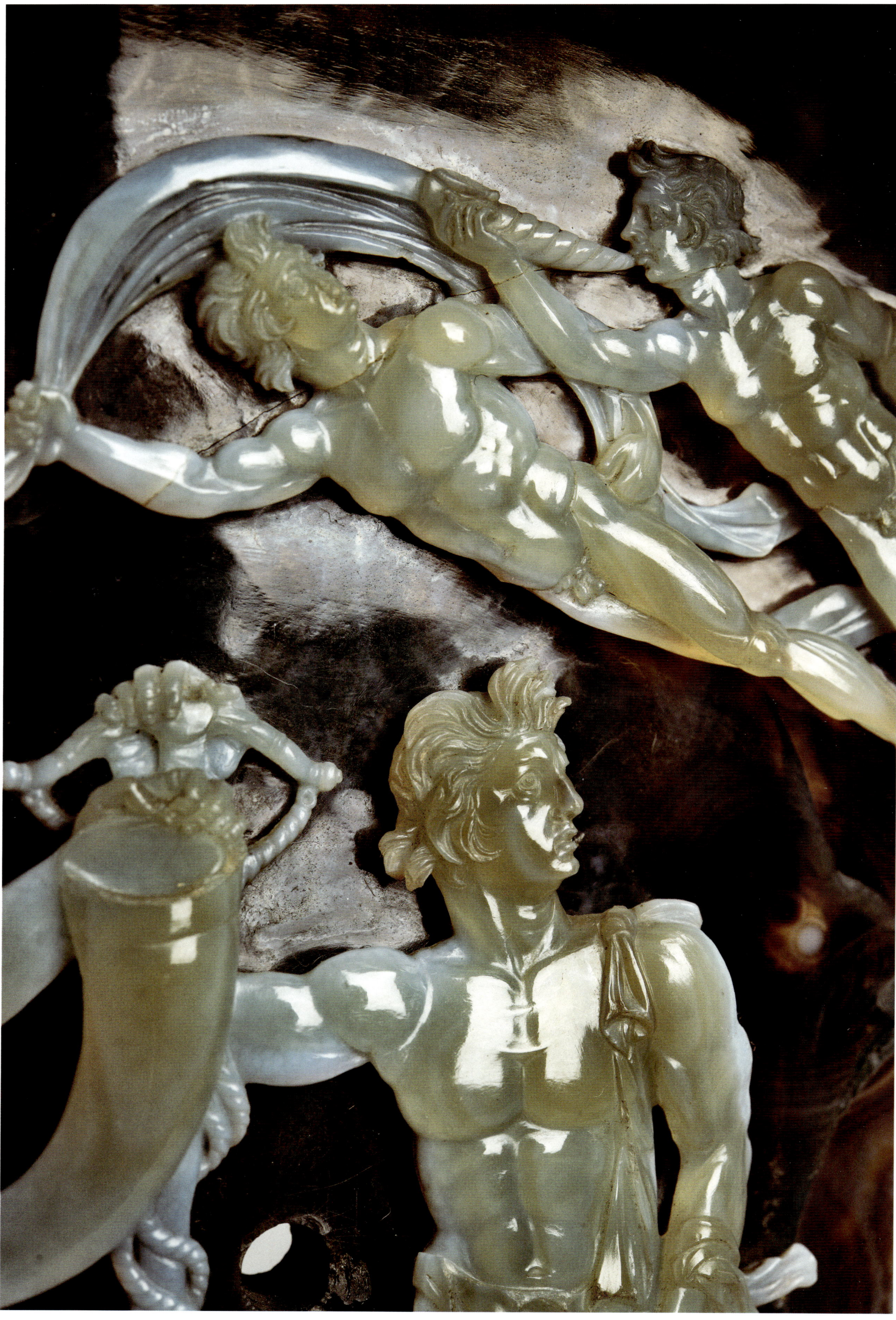

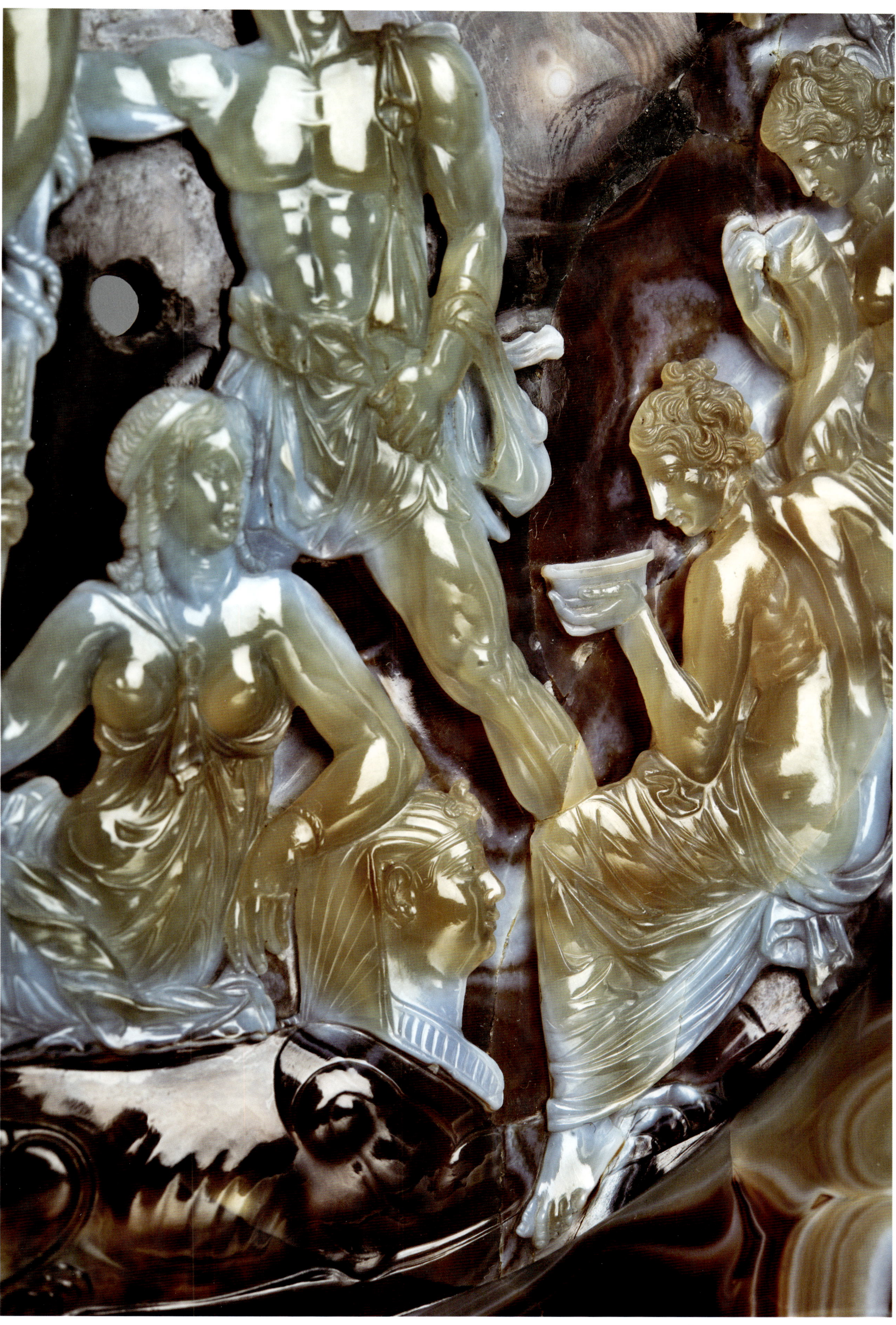

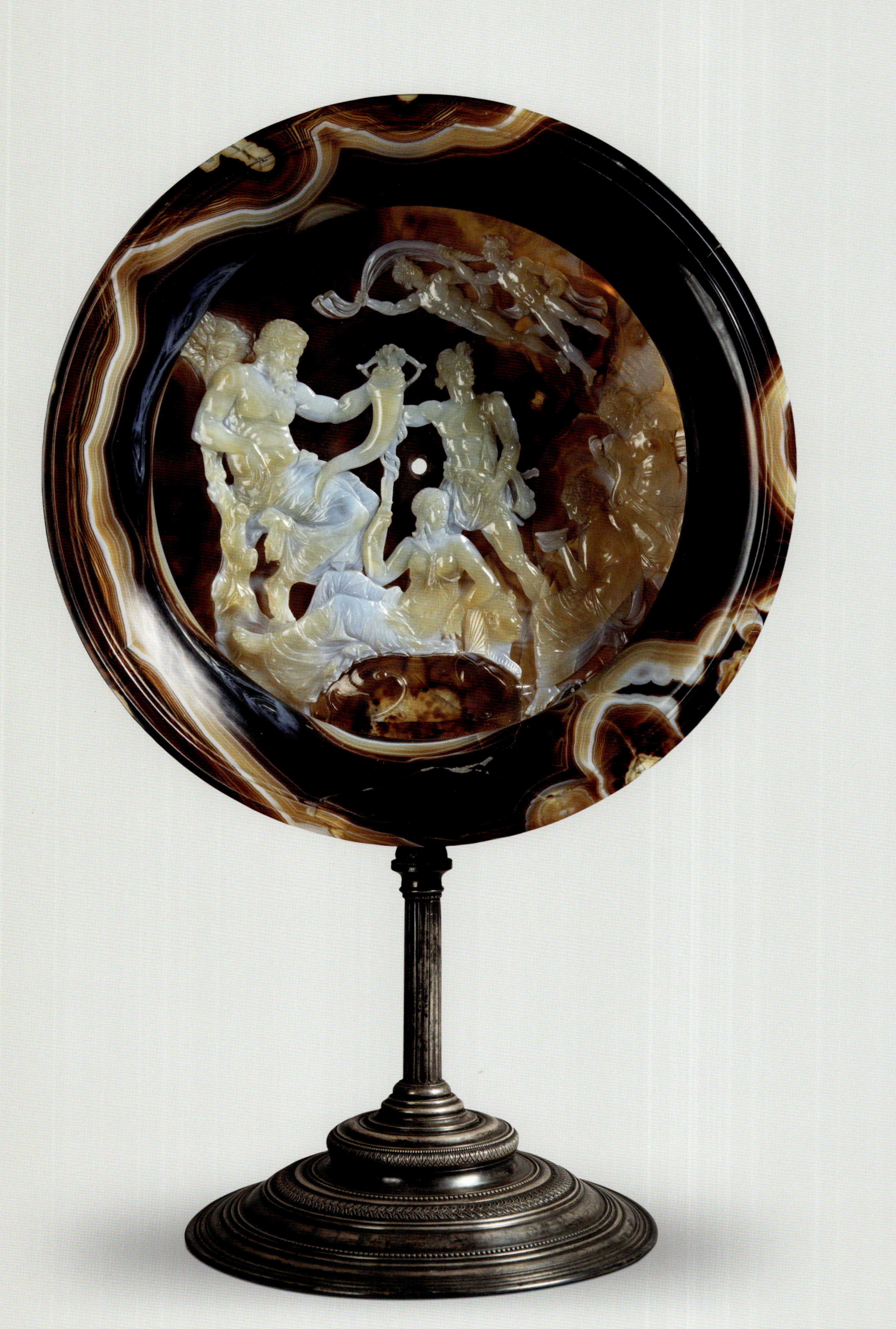

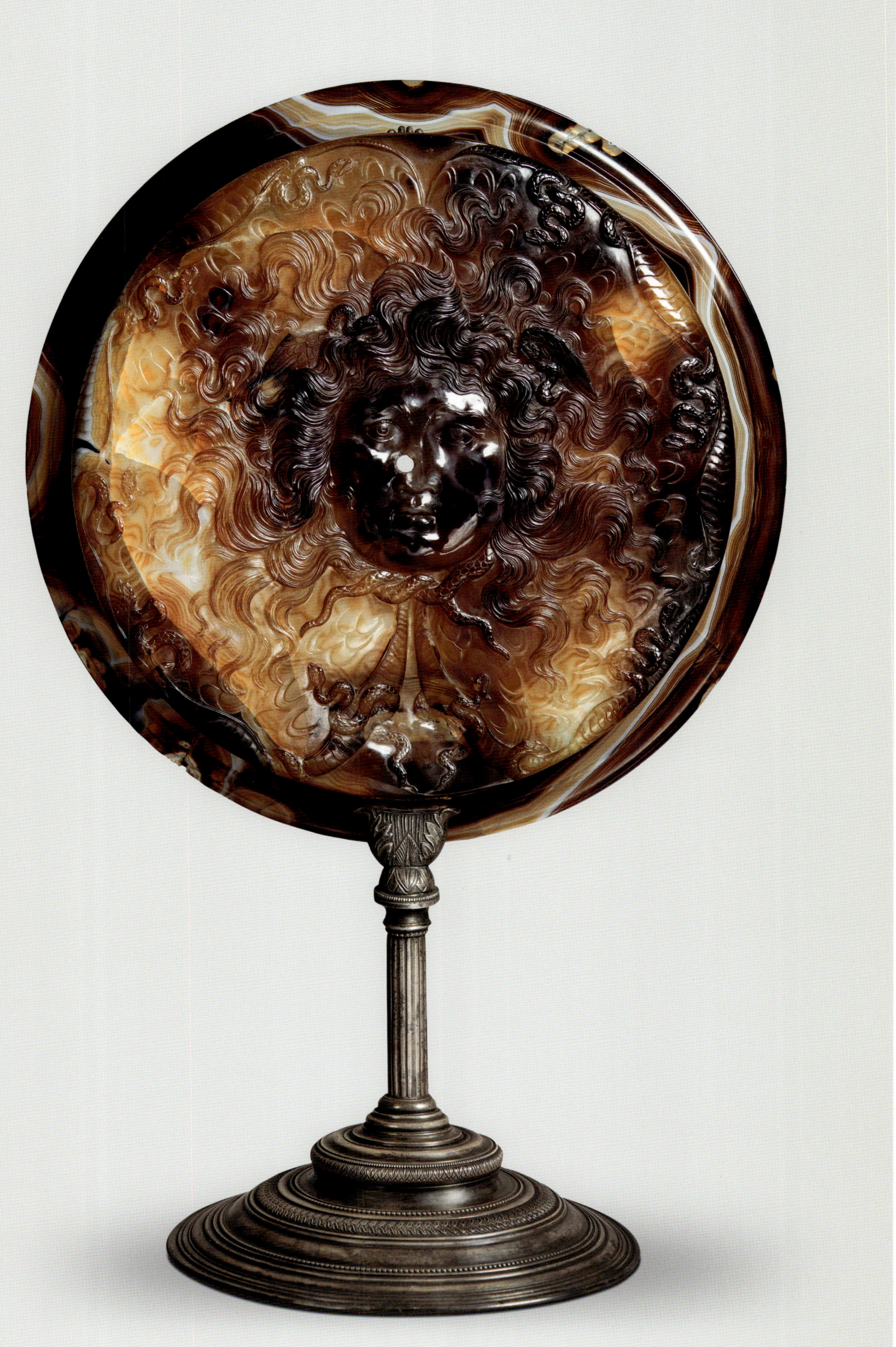

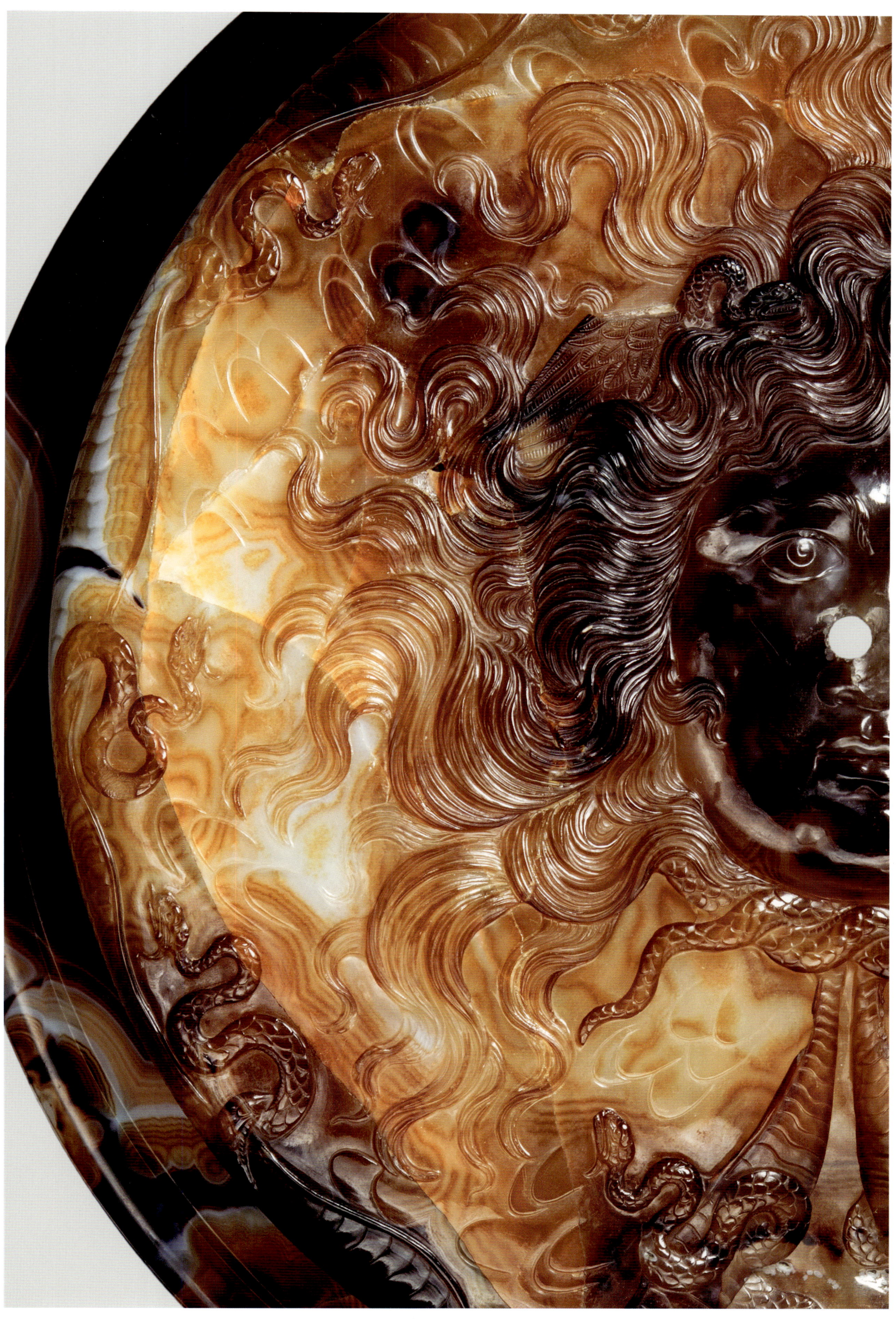

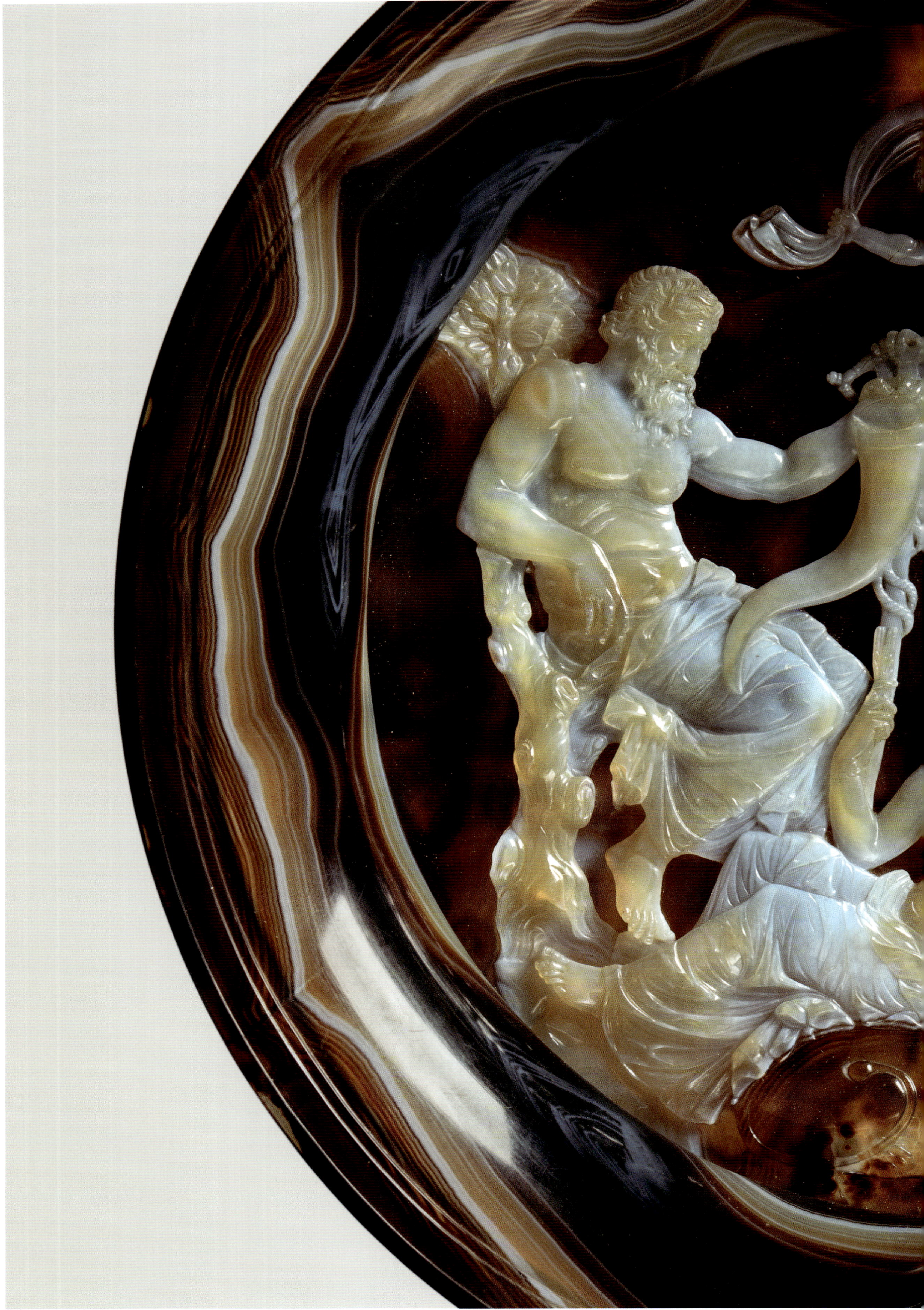

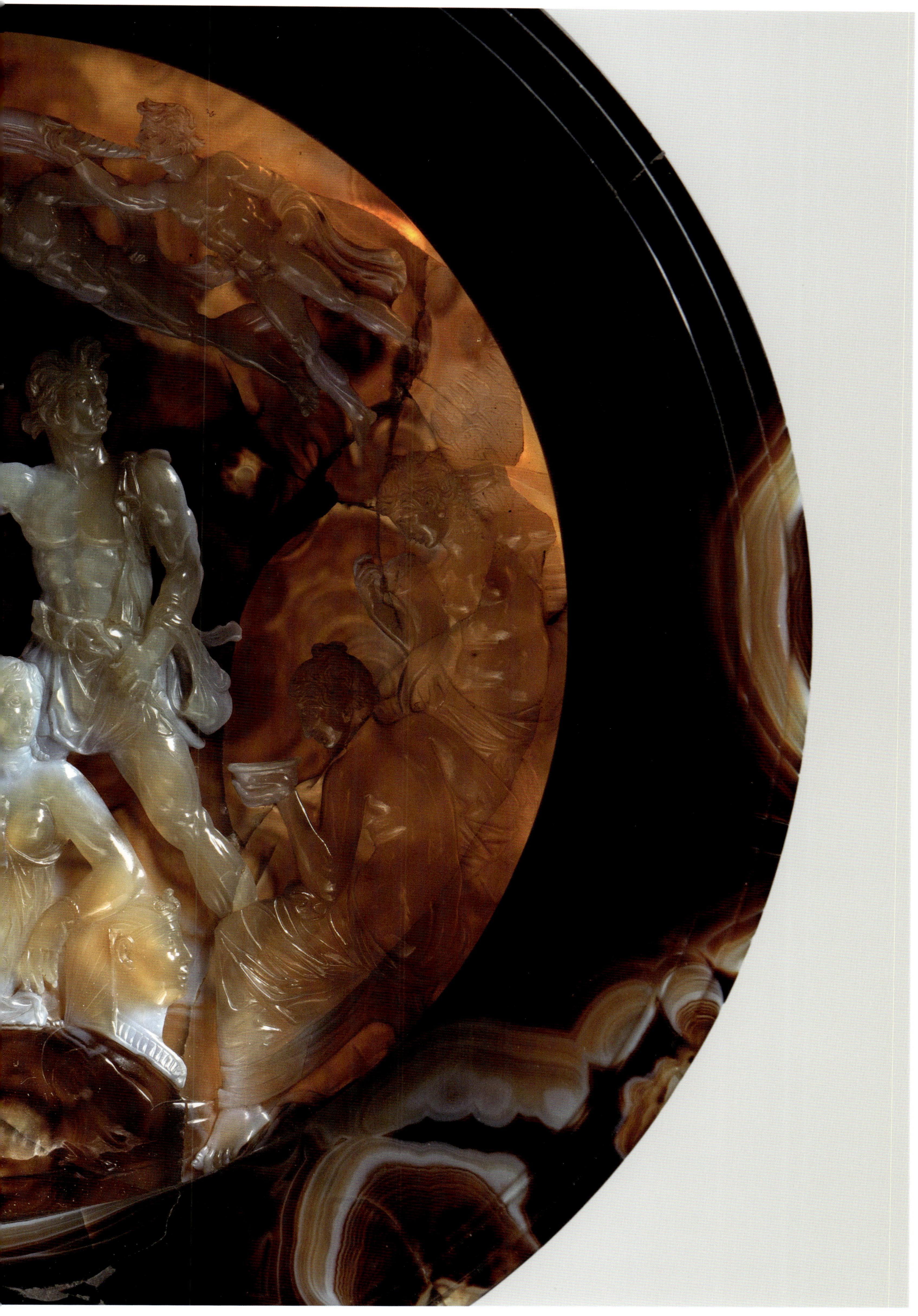

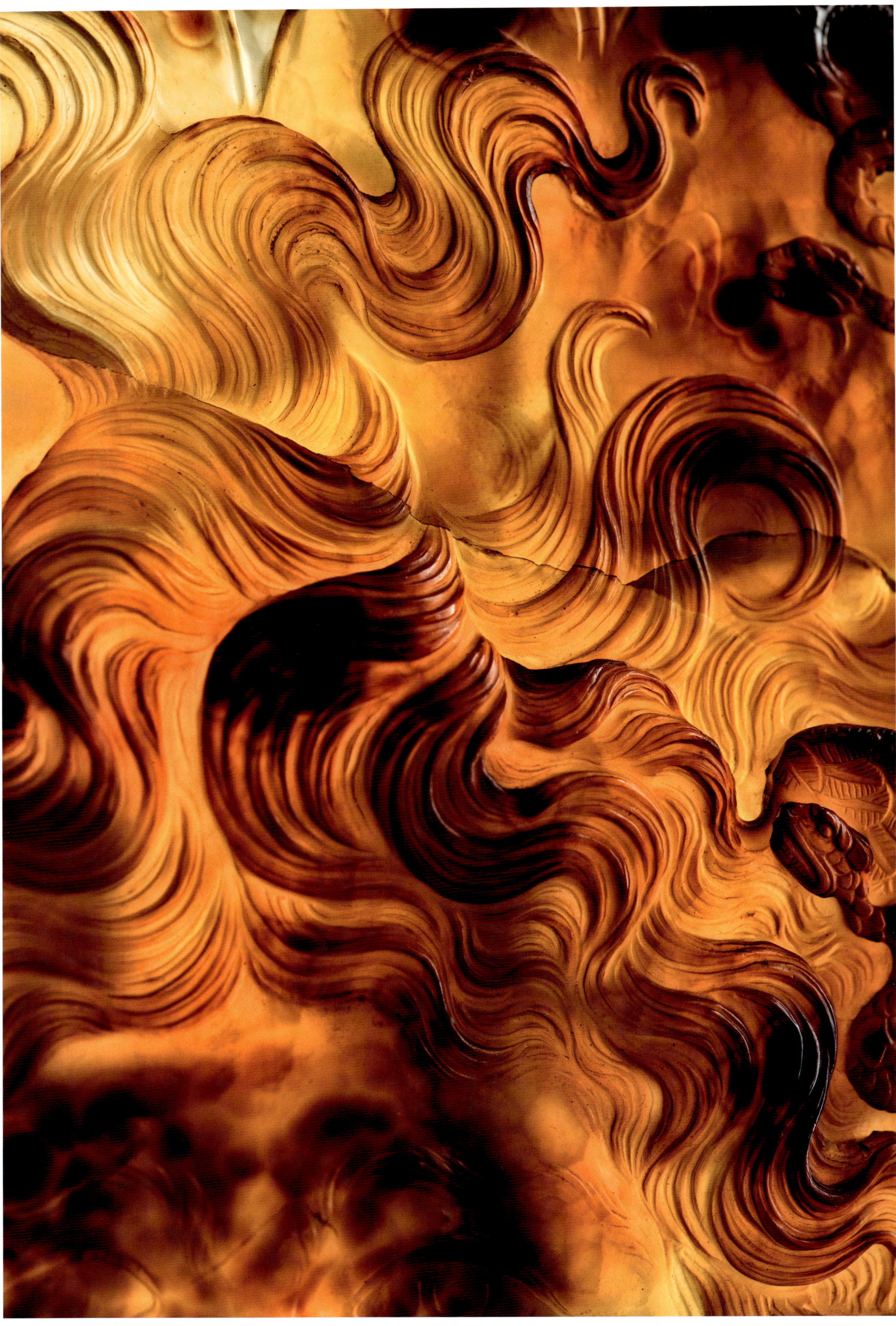

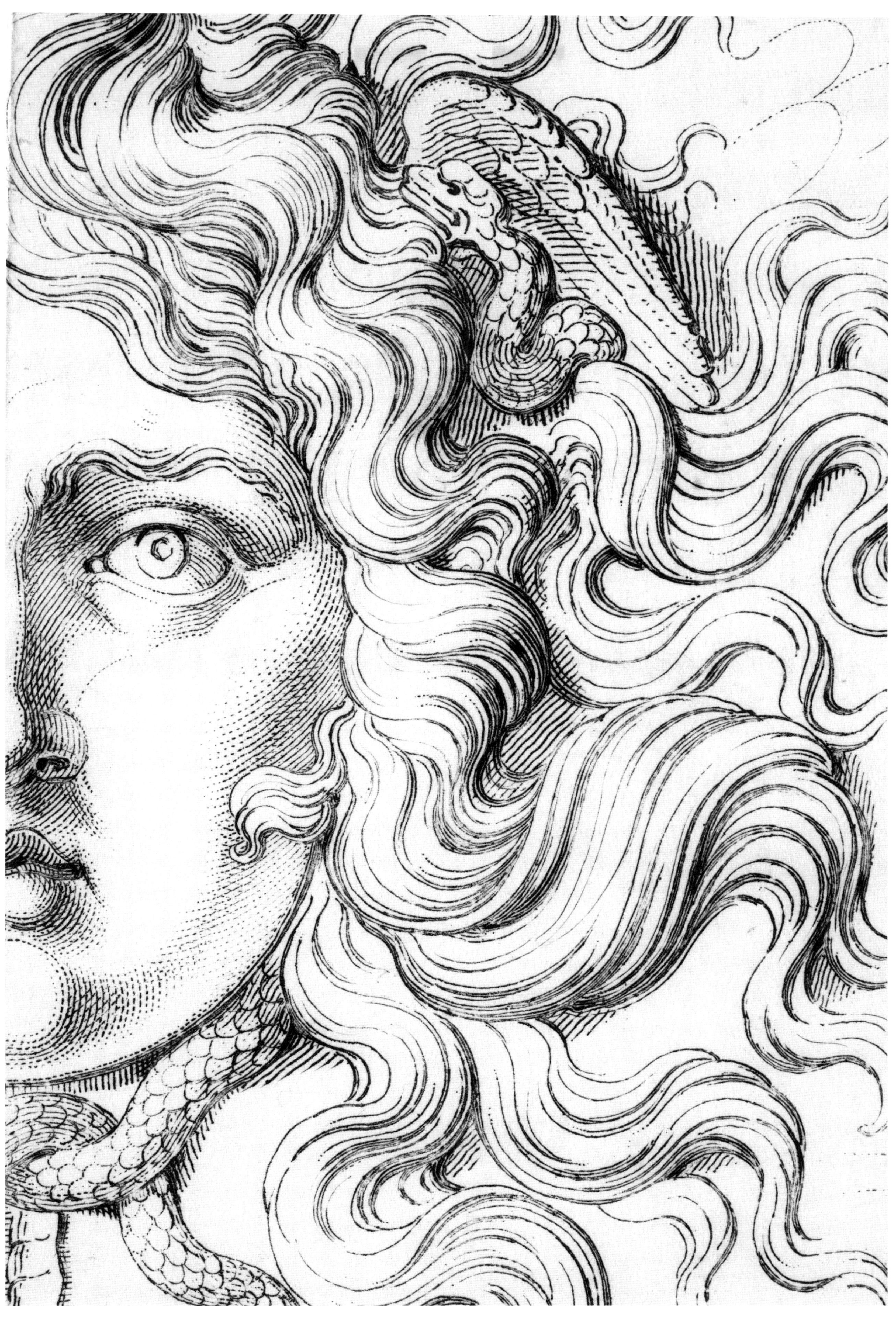

In 1471, I was appointed
ambassador to Rome
for the coronation of Pope Sixtus,
where I received many expressions
of great esteem. From here I brought
the two ancient marble heads
depicting Augustus and Agrippa,
which were gifted to me by
Pope Sixtus himself, and I brought
our engraved chalcedony bowl . . .

This reference to the purchase of the bowl known as the Farnese Cup appears in Lorenzo the Magnificent's *Ricordi*.

This was just one of the many changes of ownership that the famous artefact has experienced over its long history, during which it has never had to be dug out of the ground, unlike so many other objects from Antiquity. Commissioned by one of the rulers who succeeded Alexander the Great, the cup was engraved in Alexandria in Egypt. After Cleopatra's defeat and the consequent loss of Egyptian independence it found its way to Rome's Treasury and thence to Constantinople. This much is known because its inner decoration is the subject of a large ink drawing, now in Berlin (Blanck 1964), acquired in 1790 by the Prussian ambassador to Constantinople. The drawing was made by the Persian painter Mohammed-al-Khayyām, who lived in the early decades of the fifteenth century. He worked at the court of the Timurid ruler Baysonghur Mizra (died 1435), who had a particular fondness for graphic art, founding the Academy for the Art of Book Illustration in Herat. The handling of the figure's highly elongated eyes reveals the evident influence of Eastern art, but other aspects, such as the scene being enclosed within a circle, reproducing the shape of the artefact, the proportions of the bodies, the folds of the robes and the wholly un-Oriental composition, suggest the painter worked from the original, or at the very least from an extremely accurate copy. For this to be possible the cup would have had to be in the East and it is highly likely it remained in Constantinople until being brought back to Italy when the city at last fell to the Ottomans in 1453. Indeed, Angelo Poliziano saw it in 1458 in Naples at the court of Alfonso V of Aragon (Giuliano 1994). From there it was taken to Rome, where, as we have seen, Lorenzo de' Medici himself states he bought it in 1471. From the Florentine family's collection, in 1537 it then seems to have passed into the possession of Margaret of Austria, Charles V's natural daughter, together with a certain number of gems as part of the dower of Alessandro de' Medici, Duke of Florence. Margaret was widowed after only one year and her second marriage to Ottavio Farnese saw the treasures of the Medici's engraved gem collection, including the cup, transferred to the family of the dukes of Parma. The cup soon changed hands once again, being inherited by Charles of Bourbon, the son of Elisabetta, the last heir of the House of Farnese. As if the technical quality of its complex decoration in relief and its sheer size, which make it totally unique, were not extraordinary enough, this piece's vicissitudes as it was swapped between courts around Europe and beyond add a further intriguing layer of interest to an artefact whose raw material originally came from India.

The skilled engraver exploited the variations in the colour of the agate's multiple layers, the different tones of the chalcedony showing through in various areas, which can be seen in their natural sequence in the irregular outline on the edge of the cup, and turned them into figures ranging in colour from honey brown with red and gold shades on the outside to cerulean with pearlescent hues and gingery gold shading into reddish brown marbling on the inside.

Confident in his own ability, the artist has created an aegis (shield) on the outside with the head of Medusa at its centre. The thick, flowing locks spread over the entire surface of the skin, which is shown to be covered in scales where it is folded back on the edges, perhaps to indicate it belongs to the Giant Pallas that Athena flayed alive, then placing the head of the Gorgon in the middle; these sinuous undulations conceal the two snakes that emerge on either side of the head, as well as others depicted in varied writhing spirals around the edges, adding menace to the monstrous creature's petrifying stare. But this animal skin is also a symbol of power, the sacred royal power descended from Jupiter, and a talisman that, like Medusa, sows terror among the enemy's ranks, which is why Alexander of Macedon adopted it as his symbol and wore it into battle. Following his example, the Ptolemaic dynasty did the same in Egypt.

On the inner face a stern male figure is shown holding an empty cornucopia and sitting on the gnarled stump of a sycamore, the only tree with a woody trunk to grow in the Nile region. Next to him stands an athletic-looking young man with his hair ruffled by the wind, wearing a chiton tied at his shoulder. He holds the beam of a plough with his right hand, while his left grasps a sword emerging from the folds of a bag; in front of him a woman reclining on a sphinx raises her right hand, in which she holds two ears of wheat. Next to her are two other women, whose bodies follow the curved contours of the cup, one holding a bowl and the other an empty cornucopia. Above, the wind wafts two naked youths across the scene and causes the mantle of one to billow out, while his colleague blows on his *buccina* horn.

There have been multiple interpretations of this scene and many attempts to fathom the underlying allegorical meaning. The sphinx is the detail that immediately sets the scene in Egypt: right from the eighteenth century it has always been taken as alluding to the fertility of the Nile, represented by the seated man, and is the starting point in every explanation of the meaning of the scene. Thanks to its seasonal flooding—personified by the reclining woman, taken to be Eutheneia—the river, aided by the Etesian winds, in turn embodied by the youths drifting over the scene, ensures Egypt's prosperity (the sphinx) during the harvest seasons, symbolized by the young Horai seated at the edge of the cup, behind whom emerge ears of wheat. More recently, the woman with the cornucopia has been interpreted as representing Arura, the symbol of arable land, and the figure with the bowl as Herse, the morning dew.

On the other hand, the features of the robes worn by the woman in the centre have led some to interpret the scene as a reference to Isis's pantheon. In this reading,

Isis herself, coiffed in the style of a Ptolemaic princess, with her vestments tied in a knot between her breasts and bracelets at her wrists, reclines on a sphinx, symbolizing the rule of the Ptolemies; Osiris-Serapis is the imposing bearded deity, while the young man is their son Horos-Harpocrates. At the same time, the presence of symbols associated with the worship of Demeter and the decidedly Hellenic appearance of the actors involved means the scene can also be viewed as the result of the religious syncretism favoured by the Ptolemies, in which Isis was equated with Demeter, shown here with her husband Hades-Dionysus and Triptolemus, who, instructed by Demeter herself, was the first to grow wheat.

But the exceptional nature of this artefact—its diameter of 21 centimetres making it the largest engraved gemstone bowl of the ancient world to have survived—has led scholars since the eighteenth century to suggest it was specially commissioned by an extremely high ranking patron to celebrate a specific event. And indeed, attempts have been made to identify members of the Ptolemaic dynasty among the figures depicted. Scipione Maffei thought he detected Ptolemy Auletes with his family. Bernardo Quaranta saw the bearded figure as a representation of Ptolemy Soter, the woman as Berenice, and the standing young man as Alexander the Great himself, while Jean Chabonneaux, writing in 1958, identified the sphinx's face as the portrait of Ptolemy V Epiphanes, the young man as Horos

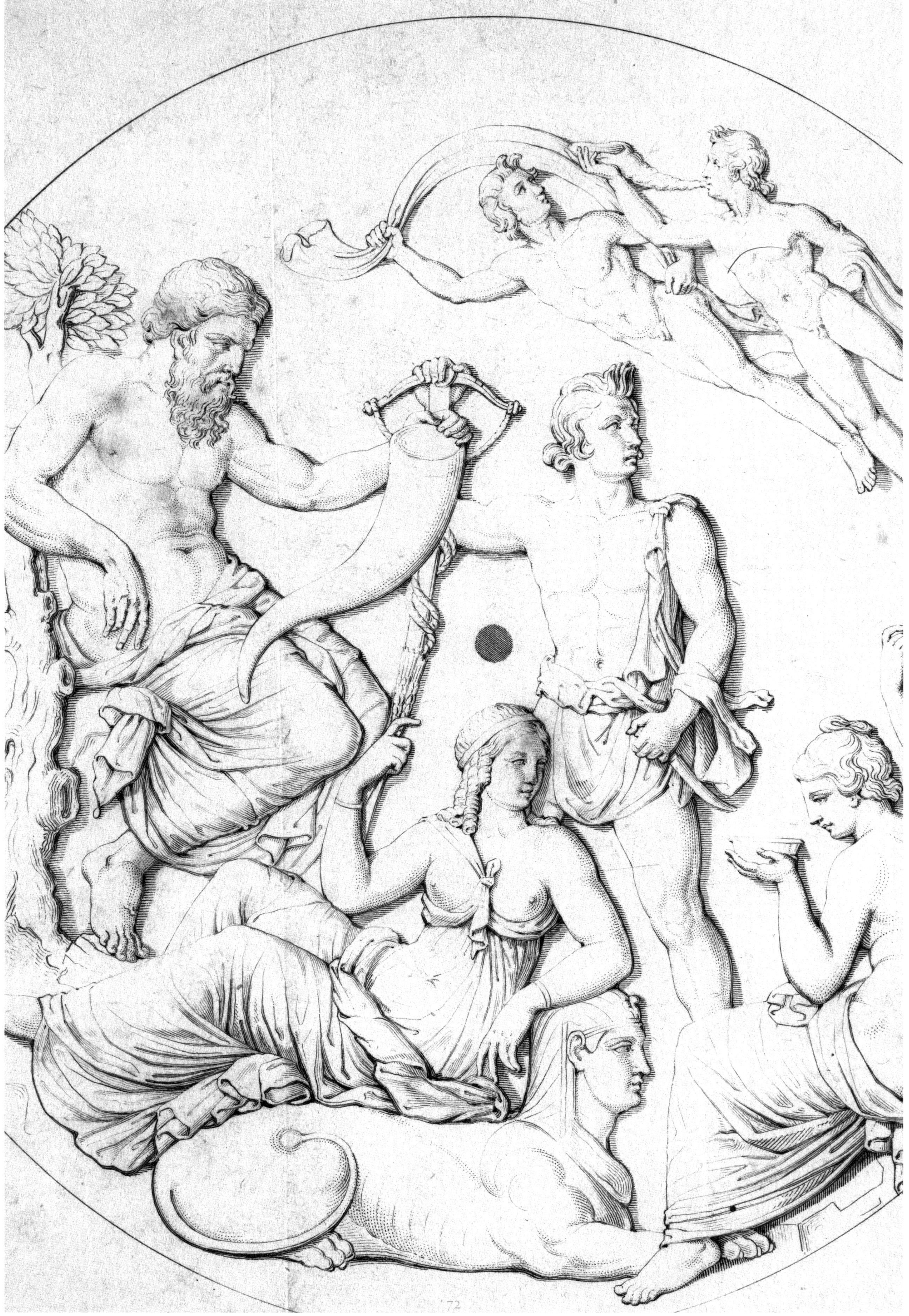

Ptolemy VI Philometor and the woman as Cleopatra I (180–173 BC). In 1962, F.L. Bastet was more inclined to see the woman as a depiction of Cleopatra III, with her son Triptolemus-Ptolemy X Alexander, who has the same typical hairstyle as his Macedonian forebear, and her husband Ptolemy VIII in the role of Osiris. The reference to the god who died and was then resurrected would fit this ruler well as he was succeeded after his death in 107 BC by his wife, on this reading depicted here with a headband, the symbol of royalty. This would imply that the cup was made after that date. Identifying the figures is thus crucial in establishing exactly when this artefact was made, but in truth neither of these points has been determined with confidence—the possible dates ranging from the third century BC to the last forty years of the first century BC. For instance, Eugenio La Rocca goes as far as to propose the period 37–34 BC, claiming that the female figure is none other than Cleopatra VII, depicted as ushering in a new period of prosperity for Egypt thanks to her understanding with Mark Antony. What is clear however is that a work of this kind must have required long and painstaking labour to create and this makes it unlikely it would have been commissioned and produced in a short time to commemorate a particular political or religious event.

A more recent reading of the scene provides a different interpretation of the standing young man, suggesting another reason for the commission of this magnificent cup. Taking his cue from previous scholars' observations, François Queyrel (2017) is convinced the figure cannot have royal status since he is not wearing the tell-tale headband and instead takes a closer look at the ethnic features that can be identified. This leads him to conclude that the figure displays many traits typical of the Galatians: the moustache (though there is actually no sign of one here), the thick hair and their considerable height. He also notes that the standing figure is wearing the short labourer's tunic and although he is holding the beam of a plough in his right hand, his left grips a sword, not a sickle, as is often thought; furthermore, he is carrying a bag of seeds. All these details identify him as a soldier-labourer. His presence in the scene completes the allegory of the rich land of Egypt, producer of multiple grain harvests, evoked by the other figures. In Ptolemaic Egypt, the *clerouchoi* were soldiers who doubled as farmers in provincial areas, and once the Galatians had been defeated by Ptolemy II in 275 BC they proved to be excellent *clerouchoi* and were rewarded with plots of land, especially in the nome (*nomos*, district) of Arsinoe, corresponding to the Fayyum area. On this reading the cup would amount to a retrospective celebration of the achievements of the reign of the ruler who first cultivated this land, naming its capital after his wife. The figures of Isis and the sphinx would thus represent Arsinoe and Ptolemy II, and the cup, for which Queyrel does not hazard a date, is actually a posthumous celebration of the couple who reigned during the Ptolemaic dynasty's golden years.

Another of the cup's outstanding distinctions is that it has survived virtually intact to the present day, as Bernardo Quaranta stresses in his long commentary on the artefact, which was added to the collection of the Real Museo Borbonico (now National Archaeological Museum of Naples) in 1817. In fact, we know it wasn't interfered with in the slightest way until the fifteenth century, since in Mohammed-al-Khayyām's drawing it is shown without the hole that was probably added later to attach a support, to the detriment of the Gorgon's face in particular. This hole was probably made by the Medici's skilled engravers, who had no qualms about adding LAV.R.MED to underline ownership even on the greatest and most beautiful ancient gems in Lorenzo the Magnificent's collection. This alteration is first mentioned in the Farnese inventory drawn up in Ortona on February 26, 1586, after Margaret of Austria's death, which reads: "An engraved, decorated agate cup, with eight figures in low relief within, and on the outer surface the head of Medusa, with a hole in the middle." This virtually unblemished condition lasted until the night between October 1 and 2, 1925, when a guard in the museum lost his head and struck the cabinet housing the work with an umbrella, breaking off the right-hand portion of the cup. The pieces were quickly collected and the restoration completed by October 11 that same year, but further work was required in 1951 to reattach pieces that had been broken off by the damp during the war.

A further peculiarity of this cup lies in the fact that it originally probably served a purely ritual purpose. The cup's shape, rather shallow and with an outward-flaring rim, would have made it difficult to use on a regular basis as a drinking vessel. Moreover, since the cup had no support, the outer decoration would have been damaged by being constantly in contact with any surface the cup rested on and the inner decoration would have been inappropriately covered by wine during a banquet. It was far more likely to have contained the libation during a religious ceremony in which only those closest to the person making the offering would have been able to see the scene depicted as the liquid was poured. *"Only the chosen few are able to understand the Cup's political message—or messages; few are invited to witness its manifestation"* (Gasparri 1994).

In the end, many were in fact privileged to see it when permitted to do so by the numerous courts that later possessed the cup and the throngs who now visit the National Archaeological Museum of Naples. Even before delving into the putative allegorical, historical and esoteric meanings that have been explored, they undoubtedly appreciate the stunning aesthetic achievement this work represents and which has remained unchanged over the years, making this the one and only "Farnese Cup."

BIBLIOGRAPHY

B. QUARANTA, "Tazza di Sardonica istoriata", in *Museo Borbonico*, vol. XII, 1839, plt. XLVII, pp. 1–34.

J. CHARBONNEAUX, "Sur la signification et la date de la Tasse Farnèse," in *Monuments Piot*, L, 1958, pp. 85-103.

F.L. BASTET, "Untersuchungen zur Datierung und Bedeutung der Tazza Farnese," in *Bullettin Antieke Beschaving*, Leiden XXXVII, 1962, pp. 1–24.

H. BLANCK, "Eine persische Pinselzeichnung nach der Tazza Farnese," in *Archäologischer Anzeiger*, 1964, pp. 307–312.

U. PANNUTI, "Tazza Farnese," in N. Dacos, A. Giuliano, U. Pannuti (eds.), *Il tesoro di Lorenzo il Magnifico. Le gemme. I*, Catalogo della Mostra Palazzo Medici Riccardi Firenze 1972, Florence 1973, pp. 69–72.

E. LA ROCCA, *L'età d'oro di Cleopatra. Indagine sulla Tazza Farnese*, Rome 1984.

A. GIULIANO, "Novità sul tesoro di Lorenzo il Magnifico," in *Lorenzo il Magnifico e il suo mondo. Atti del Convegno Internazionale di studi*, Firenze 1992, Florence 1994, p. 319.

C. GASPARRI, "'La scudella nostra di calcidonio': una Tazza per molte corti", in C. Gasparri (ed.), *Le gemme Farnese*, Naples 1994, pp. 75-83.

T. GIOVE, A. VILLONE, "Dallo Studio al Tesoro: le gemme Farnese da Roma a Capodimonte," in C. Gasparri (ed.), *Le gemme Farnese*, Naples 1994, pp. 31–57.

U. PANNUTI, "La collezione glittica medicea," in C. Gasparri (ed.), *Le gemme Farnese*, Naples 1994, pp. 61–68.

M. BARBANERA, "Alcune considerazioni su Federico II collezionista di pietre dure e sul destino della Tazza Farnese," in *Archeologia Classica* LIV, no. 4, 2003, pp. 423–441.

F. QUEYREL, "Les Galtes comme nouveaux Géants ? De la métaphore au glissement interprétatif", in F.-H. Massa-Pairault, C. Pouzadoux, *Géants et Gigantomachies entre Orient et Occident (Actes du Colloque, Naples 14-15 novembre 2013)*, Naples 2017, pp. 206–211.

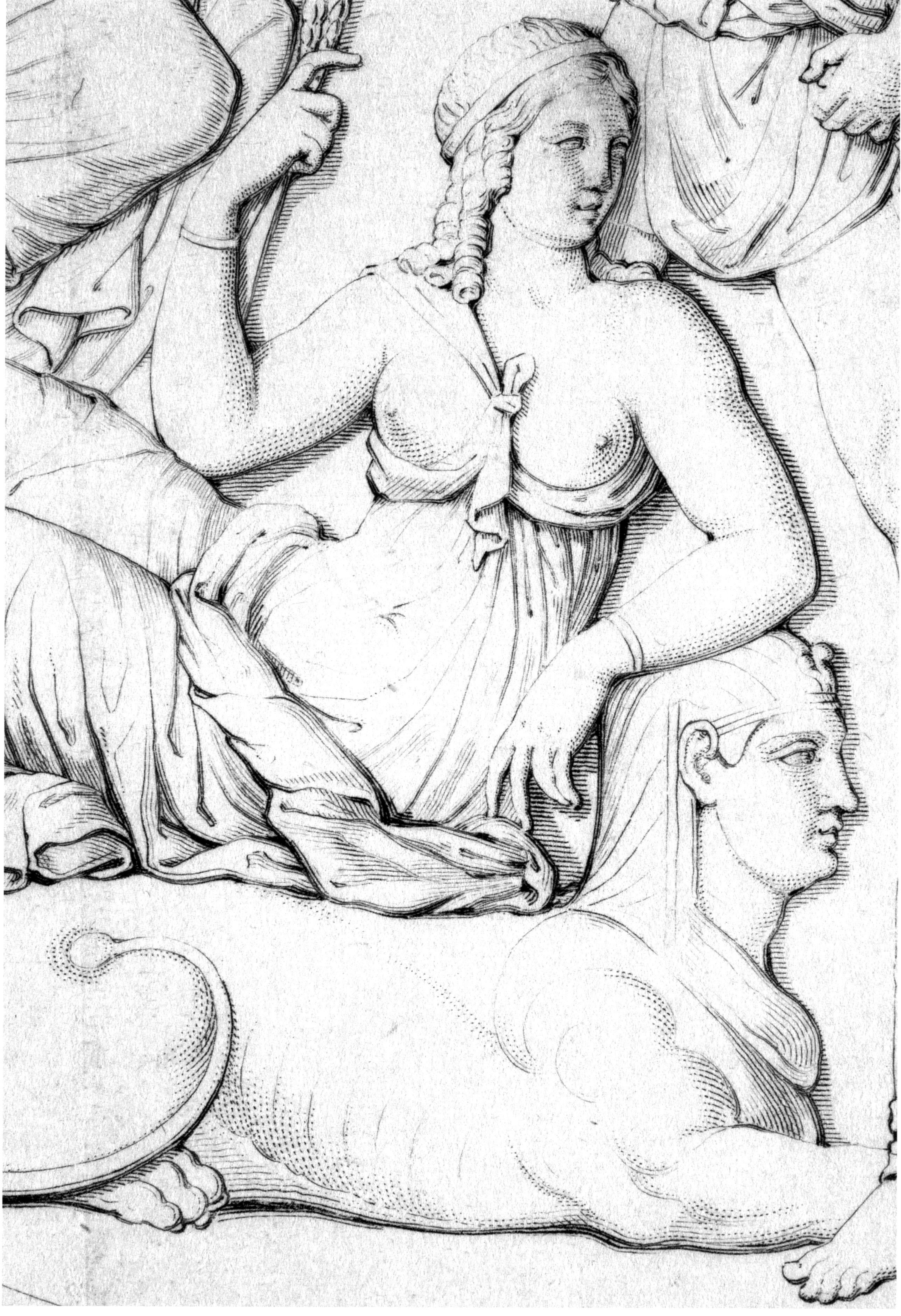

VALERIA SAMPAOLO has been conservator of the National Archaeological Museum of Naples. The author of several publications, she focuses in particular on research into the early excavations in the Vesuvius area and on establishing the provenance of the Museum's frescoes, whose new display installation she curated.

LUIGI SPINA is a photographer. His work focuses on amphitheatres and the civic dimension of the sacred, the links between art and faith, the search for ancient cultural roots, and the physical impact of classical sculpture. His published works include *L'Ora Incerta* (2014), *The Buchner Boxes* (2014), *Hemba* (2017), and *Mythical Diary* (2017). Spina has collaborated with Valeria Sampaolo and 5 Continents Editions to create the series *Oggetti rari e preziosi al museo archeologico nazionale di Napoli*, whose titles to date include *Memorie del Vaso blu* (2016), *Amazzonomachia* (2017), *Centauri* (2017), *Sette sapienti* (2018), and *Zefiro e Clori* (2018). He has also published *The Dancers at the Villa of the Papyri* for 5 Continents Editions' Tailormade series.

5 CONTINENTS EDITIONS

Editorial Coordination
Laura Maggioni

Art Direction
Annarita De Sanctis

Translations
Julian Comoy

Editing
Emily Ligniti

Colour Separation
Maurizio Brivio, Milan

Text by Valeria Sampaolo / Museo
Archeologico Nazionale di Napoli
© photographs Luigi Spina 2018
© 5 Continents Editions, Milano, 2018
for the present edition. All rights reserved

5 Continents Editions
Piazza Caiazzo, 1
20124 Milan, Italy
www.fivecontinentseditions.com

ISBN: 978-88-7439-851-5

Distributed by ACC Art Books throughout
the world, excluding Italy and Canton Ticino

Printed and bound in Italy in June 2018
by Tecnostampa, Pigini Group Printing Division
Loreto - Trevi, Italy for 5 Continents Editions, Milan

MUSEO ARCHEOLOGICO NAZIONALE
DI NAPOLI

Director
Paolo Giulierini

Valeria Sampaolo

Contracts Department
Luigi Di Caprio
Angelo Diomaiuti
Alfonso Lopez

Acknowledgments
Monica Romano
Ufficio dei Consegnatari, Museo Archeologico
di Napoli

Pages 65, 72 and 78:
Drawing and engraving by Francesco Pesante,
from *Real Museo Borbonico*,
vol. XII, Stamperia Reale, Naples 1839